W. Ron Adams

COAL MINE TO COURTROOM

A QUADRIPLEGIC'S MEMOIR OF RELENTLESS FAITH, COURAGE, AND ETERNAL SUCCESS

W. RON ADAMS
WITH FRED ANDERSON

Headline Books
Terra Alta, WV

Coal Mine to Courtroom
A Quadriplegic's Memoir of Relentless Faith, Courage, and Eternal Success

by W. Ron Adams with Fred Anderson

copyright ©2022 W. Ron Adams

To order additional copies of this book or for book publishing information, or to contact the author:

Headline Books
P.O. Box 52
Terra Alta, WV 26764
www.HeadlineBooks.com

Tel: 304-789-3001
Email: mybook@headlinebooks.com

Cover photo by Jerry Stone

ISBN 13: 9781951556730 — paperback

Library of Congress Control Number: 2021946250 — paperback

ISBN 13: 9781951556815 — hardcover

Library of Congress Control Number: 2021952706 — hardcover

PRINTED IN THE UNITED STATES OF AMERICA

In memory of my mother, Lady Ruth Adams,
and sisters, Joyce and Delores

"For I know the plans I have for you," declares the Lord, "plans to prosper you and not to harm you, plans to give you hope and a future." (Jeremiah 29:11)

TABLE OF CONTENTS

INTRODUCTION

On the night of December 10-11, 2021, a series of tornadoes caused widespread destruction and fatalities in parts of Arkansas, Missouri, Illinois, and Kentucky, including the town of Dawson Springs, Kentucky, where I spent most of my youth. Many homes and businesses were destroyed on streets where I once rode my bicycle. My heart goes out to the victims—those who survived and those who did not—and I am sad to know that many of the places I knew as a boy are gone.

Since I no longer live in Dawson Springs, the Western Kentucky tornado did not affect me personally, but what happened that night is relevant to this book because it is an example of how one's life circumstances can change in an instant, as mine did. Most day-to-day problems are relatively easy to resolve. Others are longer-lasting and can seem overwhelming. Despite the incomprehensible damage wrought by the monster twister, Dawson Springs and other towns that suffered damage will rebuild. Things will get better with time, hope, and perseverance. They did, for me.

Not to give away any big surprises, but unless you randomly stumbled across this book and started reading it without first hearing about it, you already know that I am an attorney who happens to be in a wheelchair. That, by itself, is not so unusual. The convoluted journey that brought me here is what I hope you will find interesting, informative, and maybe, occasionally, amusing.

What you are about to read is mostly accurate. I say "mostly" because a few people might disagree with my recollection of certain details. Did something happen on a Monday, or a Tuesday? How can I recall precise conversations that occurred years ago? Did I have a hidden recording device every time that I spoke with someone? Of course not. The anecdotes, quotes, and descriptions of people, places, and things in the following chapters are meant to convey a general overview of my experiences in the spirit of what happened. This is a memoir, not a trial transcript.

When I set out to tell this story, I did not want it to be a sappy, sanitized recitation of happy facts. If certain words or my descriptions of events make you cringe, I apologize in advance. My intention is not to offend readers or to air dirty laundry, but merely to tell my story as honestly as possible, warts and all. On occasion, I share unflattering details about others (and myself), but I am not seeking revenge or to embarrass anyone; I am simply relating experiences and reminiscing about people who influenced me in one way or another, for better or worse. In some cases, my opinions, as described in this book, were based on youthful ignorance or human imperfection. God has forgiven me for all kinds of transgressions, and I forgive others for theirs.

I am a Christian, but even if you do not share my beliefs, I hope that you will find other aspects of my life to be relevant to yours. We are all pretty much the same; we just come in different packages. In this book, I am honest about the progression of my faith without trying to be dogmatic. Too often, I think some Christians unwittingly put walls up that shut others out who do not agree with them. Tolerance and unconditional love are what change people, not judgmentalism. As the Greatest Person Who Ever Lived once said, "Let he who is without sin cast the first stone."

—W. Ron Adams
Author, *Coal Mine to Courtroom*

When Ron Adams invited me to collaborate on this book, I initially declined, not because I did not believe in his story but because I believed it to be so compelling I felt he would be better served by someone who had more experience writing other people's memoirs. To expose another person's imperfect life accurately would need to be done delicately, without crossing the fine line between total truth and questionable taste. Despite my resistance, Ron insisted he wanted to work with me because I already knew so much about him and he was comfortable discussing deeply personal issues with me. I kept arguing against my involvement, but like any good lawyer, he had a strong rebuttal. Finally, he prevailed.

I met Ron in 2008 through a mutual friend, Ruth Reyer, who was the development director for his law firm. I had known Ruth for many years, having worked with her and her late husband on some projects for an advertising agency and, later, a sports apparel company they owned. One day, she asked me to write a brochure for Ron's firm, consisting of a two-page mini-biography. As Ron and I became acquainted, I grew to admire him for his tenacity, generosity, and self-confidence. As I soon discovered, condensing such a complex life story to two pages was a difficult challenge, and the required brevity did not do it justice. I am now glad to have more pages to work with

Coal Mine to Courtroom touches on many things. It is about a debilitating physical condition, but it is not a medical book. It mentions certain aspects of law, but it is not a legal textbook. It discusses religion but does not proselytize. There are other books for those purposes. This one is simply the true story of an extraordinary person who has endured seemingly impossible challenges while never losing his sense of humor or his faith.

Ron Adams is one of the most fascinating people I have ever met. The experiences described and opinions expressed in this book are his alone, told from his point of view. It was my honor to help organize and shape them in a way that we hope will entertain and inspire.

—Fred Anderson
Co-author, *Coal Mine to Courtroom*

1

Prologue: Into the Dark

Even before that day, when my life changed forever, I hated the job.

There was nothing to like about coal mining, except the money. The work was dirty, dark, and dangerous. You never knew when the ceiling might collapse, crushing you in an instant under tons of rubble or trapping you for who-knows-how-long, or when you might asphyxiate from carbon monoxide, or when a spark might ignite a pocket of methane gas and blow everyone to smithereens. Of course, there was also the inescapable coal dust, perpetually lingering in the air. No matter how thoroughly you covered your nose and mouth with rags, it got into your nostrils, throat, and lungs. Respirators were not ordinarily used because coal dust would clog the filters and get all over the facepiece, obscuring a miner's vision. Whenever I ventured underground, I thought about how many men and women had died from black lung disease through the years and how their families had suffered. No doubt, coal mining would kill you one way or another if you stuck with it long enough, which I had no intention of doing. This was just temporary, a way to make money for college. I was going to get out while I was young.

Eastern Kentucky is the part of the state more commonly associated with "black gold," but the far western region also has rich coal deposits which, for many years, provided steady work for those brave enough—or desperate enough—to do it.

There surely was plenty of desperation in my town, where job opportunities were in short supply and men had young mouths to feed.

One hundred-sixty miles southwest of Louisville, Dawson Springs felt like the middle of nowhere. The surrounding area consisted of mostly farms, forests, and hills riddled with coal mines. I worked sixty miles to the north in Uniontown, near the Ohio River, in Hamilton Mine No. 2, which the Island Creek Coal Company owned.

I commuted to work each day, scrunched into the rear compartment of a Chevy Suburban with four other miners—two in the front and two in the backseat. We carpooled to save money on gas, but I hated the ride. I was nineteen, and the other guys were twenty or thirty years older. We had nothing in common except coal. They cussed a lot and talked about women and drinking and they listened to country music on the radio, which I found irritating. I didn't dislike all country music, just the twangy, honky-tonk kind, because it was what my dad listened to at home. But the worst part of my daily commute was the nauseating cigarette smoke that filled the vehicle on cold days when the windows were rolled up. By the time I arrived at work, my lungs were already polluted and my eyes burned. Going into the mine seemed almost like a breath of fresh air.

The temperature in a coal mine is determined by several factors, including depth and latitude. Mines close to the Equator can be 85 degrees or thereabouts. The air in Kentucky mines is about fifty-five degrees, year-round. Except for the general nastiness of the underground environment, a mine is quite comfortable—nice and cool in the summer and relatively warm during the winter. Like most miners, I wore coveralls, steel-toe work boots, and a safety helmet with a light mounted on the front.

Underground mines (as opposed to open-pit and strip mines) are laid out in a grid-like fashion with multiple, parallel tunnels intersecting at a ninety-degree angle, like a series of one-way streets in a city's downtown, allowing equipment to move in and out freely. Though mining technology has improved, the basic process of building underground coal mines has not changed much since the late 1800s. Tunnels are still blasted with explosives, after which miners go in and start digging with picks, shovels, and machines, scooping chunks of coal into minecarts. In the old days, donkeys or mules would pull the carts out on tracks. In the 1920s and 1930s, motorized carts began to replace animals working in coal mines, leaving humans as the remaining beasts of burden.

On the morning of Thursday, March 17, 1977, my supervisor told me I would have to fill in for another worker whose job was driving a machine called a shuttle car. The other guy had called in sick, which probably meant he was hungover. In those days, drinking was common among the miners, sometimes even on the job.

I had a general understanding of how a shuttle car worked, but I had not been trained properly and was not supposed to operate one. It was probably a violation of OSHA (Occupational Safety and Health Administration) regulations, but that did not seem to matter to my boss. He needed someone to do the job that day, and I did not want to cause trouble by refusing.

A shuttle car is a seventeen-ton, motorized bin, about ten feet wide and sixteen feet long, that transports coal through the mine and dumps it onto a conveyor, which carries the coal the rest of the way out. The operator steers while seated in a small, open-air compartment. A giant spool on the shuttle car reels a 440-volt DC cable in and out as needed to power the motor.

Another big machine called a continuous miner is always moving ahead of the shuttle cars. The continuous miner has a 500-pound rotating head—a tungsten-steel cylinder covered with square-shaped protrusions that look like giant teeth— which grinds away at the ceiling, causing chunks of coal to fall. Robotic gathering arms scoop up the broken coal and dump it onto a conveyer in the rear of the continuous miner, which, in turn, dumps the coal into a shuttle car. Multiple shuttle cars run simultaneously; as one picks up a load of coal, others are hauling theirs away.

The constant grinding and scooping of coal permeates the air with thick, choking dust that stings the eyes, seeps into a miner's pores, and clings to his hair. To reduce the coal dust in the air, mines are designed with multiple entrances and fans that constantly suck fresh air in from the surface and blow it out through various exit points. Sprinklers mounted on the head of the continuous miner spray a watery mist to make the dust particles settle more quickly, but it's never enough. Visibility is poor during this part of the mining process.

"Oh, my God, this is so nasty and disgusting," I thought. *"Why on earth am I here?"*

Adding to the surreal atmosphere were plastic curtains that hung from ceiling to floor and from wall to wall, every few yards, to further minimize the spread of coal dust. The curtains were necessary but also hazardous because they could grab onto anything loose as a shuttle car passed through them. Drivers were taught to keep their heads down to avoid snagging their hardhats.

I had just picked up a load of coal two miles inside the mine and was driving through one of the cross-cut tunnels to empty the load onto a conveyer one hundred yards away. The tunnel was about four and a half feet high, so I was already hunched over, but as I approached a plastic curtain, I ducked down even lower. What I did not realize, and could not see, was that the ceiling on the other side was about a foot lower than normal because it had not been cut properly. At the same time, the shuttle car started to climb a few inches higher as it rolled over coal debris that remained on the floor.

As the shuttle car emerged on the other side of the curtain, I started to raise up, but my visibility was obscured by the dusty fog, which was so thick I could not even see my lap. Suddenly I heard my helmet scraping and realized I was about to become wedged between the ceiling above me and the machine beneath me. Space in the driver's compartment was tight. To bend down, I had to tuck my left leg under my body. I lowered my head as much as possible and tried to reach the brake pedal with my right foot, but things were happening too fast. Even though the shuttle car was moving slowly, there was no stopping it. The ceiling was getting lower and I had nowhere to go. My hard hat scraped the ceiling again. Then came a horrific popping sound in my neck, like firecrackers. I was being crushed like a cockroach under a shoe.

In that split-second, I must have passed out, because I don't remember falling out of the shuttle car. I woke up face-down on the tunnel floor, next to the shuttle car, which had come to a complete stop, jammed into a space where the ceiling was too low for it to continue. The electric motor was still humming.

I tried to get up, but I could not move my arms or legs. *"What in the world is going on?"* I thought. It was the scariest moment of my life. At first, excruciating pain shot through my body like bolts of lightning, but then numbness began to set in. I cried and yelled for help. Pounding, mechanical noises that emanated from distant reaches of the mine grew quiet as equipment started shutting down. Even if other miners could not hear me shouting, they must have realized something was wrong because I had not returned with a load of coal within the usual timeframe.

"Hey, Ronnie, what happened?" came a frantic voice. One of my coworkers had found me. "Are you okay?"

"I don't know," I moaned. "I think I'm hurt bad."

Over the next few minutes, more people arrived. Very carefully, they rolled me onto my side and slid a stretcher underneath me, then gently laid me back down on it and lifted me into a rescue cage that could be placed on a supply cart to take me out of the mine. As they carried me, everything was a blur. I was confused, drifting in and out of consciousness. Despite the darkness of that hellhole, one fact was as plain as the light of day—I could not move a muscle and everything below my neck was numb. I felt absolutely no pain. I wished I could.

2

BLACK AND WHITE
AND POOR ALL OVER

I don't know why so many people in my town ended up working in coal mines instead of trying for something better. Maybe because they grew up without role models who went to college. In some cases, it might have been because they married young, or not at all, and had to support a family.

Don't get me wrong—I have the highest respect for coal miners, in general. They have played a crucial role in America's economic development and improvements in almost everyone's quality of life for over a century. But the way many coal companies have historically treated their workers has been despicable, from shameful living conditions in company towns to lack of safety enforcement, union-busting, and even in some cases, murder[1]. Growing up, I had no intention of staying in Uniontown any longer than necessary. Or Dawson Springs. Or any of the other little towns where I bounced around as a child and where the coal company controlled everything.

I was born Walter Ronald Adams in 1957, in Morganfield, Kentucky, but spent my first six years in St. Charles, about fifty miles away. I was named after my father, Walter Morris Adams, but my mom gave me the middle name Ronald because Ronald Reagan was one of her favorite actors. Mom stood five feet, one

---

1   Lorraine Boissoneault, "The Coal Mining Massacre America Forgot", *Smithsonian Magazine*, April 25, 2017

inch tall, and weighed one hundred-fifteen pounds. Her name was Lady Ruth Adams, but she hated being called "Lady," so she went by "Ruth." As a boy, whenever I wanted to tease her, I called her "Lady," which aggravated her, but I thought it was funny.

In St. Charles, we lived in a small frame house with siding made of cheap roll roofing material, junk cars on cinder blocks in the front yard, old tires leaning against the wall, and no indoor plumbing. We drew water from a well and used an outhouse to relieve ourselves, never considering the potential health hazard of drinking from one hole in the ground and pooping into another one nearby.

When I was seven, we moved to Uniontown, into a cinderblock house, which was a step up from our previous one, but still just as ugly. Like most of the other houses in town, ours was owned by the coal company. At least we had indoor plumbing for the first time in my life, but the city shut off our water because Dad had not paid the bill. For the next few weeks, twice a week, Mom and I rode with him to a park over in Morganfield, seven miles away, where he filled a garbage can with water from a public faucet. Dad heaved the garbage can into the trunk of the car, tied the lid down, and we drove home. That's how we got our drinking water until Dad paid the city what he owed. As you might imagine, baths were rare, but Mom scrubbed me with a washcloth and soap every day until my elbows were raw.

"We may be poor, but we're not gonna be dirty," she always said.

Some people have trees in their backyard. We had grain silos—giant tanks filled with tons of mostly corn and soybeans waiting for distribution by train or truck. Sometimes, the grain emitted a sour-smelling, toxic gas as it started to ferment. As far as I know, it never made us sick, but it could have killed us if the breeze had blown just right, while the windows were open.

The silos attracted thousands of sparrows, which attracted me with my BB gun. Do you know what kind of mess that many birds can make flying over your house all the time? In the summer, I would shoot at them. Usually, the BBs would just "ding" as they bounced off the silos, causing huge flocks of sparrows to suddenly flutter away in a dark cloud of flapping wings, but sometimes I hit my target. Over two summers, I probably killed about fifteen or twenty birds. I always felt guilty, but then I would do it again. It seemed like fun. I can't explain it. Why do gambling addicts keep gambling, even though they lose money? I suppose it's human nature to do what feels good and worry about the consequences later.

We didn't have too many nice things, but we did have a black-and-white television. I liked to watch *Mutual of Omaha's Wild Kingdom* and *Gilligan's Island*. (In case you're wondering, I preferred Mary Ann because she was perky, pretty and nice, like the girl next door. Ginger was too pretentious and self-centered, for my taste.) On Saturday mornings, I watched cartoons. My favorite was *Rocky and Bullwinkle*. My overall favorite show was *Walt Disney's Wonderful World* every Sunday night. I loved shows that took my youthful imagination to other parts of the world.

We were poor white trash. When I was about ten years old, I was invited to another kid's birthday party over on the nice side of town, but I couldn't afford a present. When I showed up empty-

The house in Uniontown, Kentucky, where Ron lived at age 7.

handed, the maid asked me to leave. It bothered me for a while, but then I forgot about it because I didn't know the birthday boy very well. I had more important things to worry about than what some snobby rich people thought about me.

There wasn't much to do in Uniontown. Basketball was a big deal. I remember the first time I watched our grade school team play when I was in the fourth grade. Admission was ten cents. I had two dimes, so I could afford the game ticket and a bag of popcorn and a Coke. The hustle and bustle around the gym was so exciting—all the cheering and the pageantry. For a poor kid in a small Kentucky town, it was so cool!

I came from a blended family. My mom met my dad in the early 1950s, but she had been married once before, in 1933, at the age of fifteen. She had three daughters. The first one, Mary Lou, died from whooping cough, then came Joyce in 1935 and Delores in 1938. All that time, Mom's first husband ran around and chased women.

Meanwhile, Mom's father—my grandfather—was a moonshiner. It was the Great Depression and everyone was just trying to survive. Unfortunately, Grandpa got caught and spent a year in prison. Then, when the girls—my half-sisters— were about four and six years old, their dad—my mom's first husband—was killed in a car wreck in Cadiz, Kentucky, near what is now Land Between the Lakes State Park. The way I heard it, he and some friends were out drinking and riding around in a convertible and got going too fast to make a turn. I don't know if they were drinking Grandpa's hooch, but after all the bad things that had happened, it's easy to see why Mom never liked being around alcohol. For her, it was a never-ending source of pain, problems, and poverty.

The accident left Mom single with two small girls. To make ends meet, she waited tables, and when World War II started, she took a second job as a welder, like many other women did back then. Mom was an honest-to-goodness "Rosie the Riveter!"[2] She always had a strong work ethic and was the backbone of the

---

2   "Rosie the Riveter" was a character in an advertising campaign to recruit
women to work in the defense industry during World War II, while many men
were overseas, fighting the war.

family before I was born and throughout my life.

My older half-sister, Joyce, got pregnant at sixteen, married her boyfriend, and moved to Dawson Springs, about sixty miles south of Uniontown. Mom's other daughter, Delores, was seventeen when Mom met my father. As soon as Delores graduated from high school, she got married and moved into the apartment next to my mom and dad, in the duplex where they were living at that time. Mom was almost forty when she gave birth to me.

I developed a close relationship with Delores because she lived next door and I saw her all the time. I called her "Lolo." I loved following her around, and she would let me sit in her lap while she was pregnant with twins. That bond lasted into adulthood and helped balance out the bad stuff in my life. I was sad when she and Richard moved away to Kansas City, but I still saw them about once a year when they came back to visit.

With Delores and Joyce off on their own, it was just my mom, my dad, and me. Dad worked in a coal mine, like most of the other men in town. The first few years he and Mom were together, I don't think he drank much. Mom would not have married him if he did, but that would change after I came along.

Dad had been married once before. He had a son, who would have been my half-brother, but he died at age three. Dad also had a daughter named Sherry, but they were estranged, so he didn't really have a family of his own. According to Mom, after she and Dad got married, he wanted to have a son, but things started to go downhill after I was born. My guess is he got used to being the center of attention during their first four years of marriage, but when I came along, I started getting the lion's share of Mom's affection. I think Dad felt left out—maybe a little jealous—and started to drink more and more.

Dealing with an alcoholic is like handling dynamite—any little thing can trigger an explosion. Every moment my dad was in the house, it seemed as if there was getting ready to be a problem of some kind, especially if he was drunk.

When I was real young—about two years old—Dad used to grab me by the arm and kick me in the butt if I stepped in front of the TV while he was watching it. One Saturday morning, after I had just started walking, Mom and Lolo went shopping and left me at home with Dad. I did not remember this until it was told to me years later, but Mom cautioned Dad to keep an eye on me because I had figured out how to open the front door. When Mom and Lolo returned, the door was wide open, Dad was asleep on the couch, and I was gone. He had been drinking. They found me stumbling along the railroad tracks near our house fifteen minutes later.

Dad did not just drink at home; sometimes he drank at work, underground. Most of the time, however, he boozed it up with his friends. Usually, he would come home around 6:00 p.m., scarf down his dinner, and then head straight over to the pool hall, his favorite hangout. He almost always came home drunk, around midnight.

When I got a little older, it was my job to take the trash out to a steel barrel and burn it. The trash was always full of Dad's empty half-pint whiskey bottles. One of his favorite brands was Heaven Hill. As far as I was concerned, it should have been called "Having Hell" because it turned him into a demon. I hated those bottles so much because of what they represented; I would take rocks and break them into pieces.

Looking back, I am amazed that Dad managed to work as much as he did, considering how much he drank. At least he wasn't lazy, but in spite of all the hours he put in at the mine, there was never enough money. I can remember many times Mom putting me in the car and driving sixty miles just to get a cash advance of fifteen or twenty dollars. The way it worked was this…

There was a store owned and operated by the coal company, which was basically a general store that sold groceries, clothing, and other essentials. It was a typical "company store," the kind of which were common in most coal towns. In the store, there was a window where Mom would get coupons worth a certain amount of money, which came out of my dad's pay. Then, we would walk over to a guy sitting in a corner who gave Mom sixteen dollars in cash for twenty dollars' worth of coupons. It was a total rip-off, but if you worked for the coal company, you had to play by their rules. We went through the cash-advance scam at least once a month, all because Dad wasted so much money on liquor. It just goes to show how insidious alcoholism is.

Uniontown was a very segregated community. One half was nicknamed "White Town" and the other half was "Black Town." In between was a somewhat integrated area where we lived. We were more toward Black Town than the all-white section, if that tells you anything.

Despite the segregation, I didn't feel that there was any real racism—at least, not the hateful kind, and certainly not among the kids. Everyone got along pretty well. Most of my black friends went to the Catholic school. I went to a public school. I was in the second grade the first time a black kid started going to my school, but if there were any racial issues, I wasn't aware of them. Kids have to be taught to be racist, and despite the many problems in my family, that was not one of them.

One of the few nice things my dad ever did for me was to put up a basketball goal in our backyard when I was about twelve. There was no pavement, just dirt, but I was suddenly real popular with a lot of black kids who lived nearby. Several of them played with me every day, so long as the yard wasn't muddy. One time, I said to my grandmother, "Us colored boys have fun out there, playing basketball." I didn't mean it as a racist comment. It was just that sometimes I was the only white kid playing against ten or twelve black kids. They were my friends. We were all the same as far as I was concerned, with one exception—they were better at basketball. That's how I got good at the game. I was playing against harder competition.

Ron, age 5, sitting on a well in his grandmother's backyard.

3

BIRDS, BEES, AND BUNNIES

I don't remember exactly when I first learned about sex, but I remember the time I discovered I could make money by letting rabbits do what they do best.

My first business venture involved me and one of my black friends, Henry McQuire. He had three brothers and a sister and they lived a block closer to White Town than I did. One summer, we built a rabbit cage and a little fenced-in place in Henry's backyard. We pooled our money and bought a couple of rabbits to make more rabbits and sell them. Every day, we cleaned up the poop and put out fresh straw. Sure enough, it wasn't long before the female was pregnant. The first indication of her impending motherhood was when she grew extra fur under her chin and started pulling it out to make a nest for her babies. We didn't have a clue about the gestation period, so we didn't know when the bunnies were due, but the mama rabbit was getting bigger and bigger. We were so excited.

About 6:30 one evening, Henry knocked on my front door. I was home with Mom. Dad had already come in from work, eaten dinner, and gone to the pool hall.

"The rabbit's having her babies!" Henry said. "Come on!"

"Ronnie, you know your daddy will be angry if he comes home and you're not here," Mom said.

"He never comes back till bedtime," I pleaded. "Can't I go? I want to see the babies!"

After giving it some thought, she relented: "All right, but hurry back."

I jumped on my bike and raced the two blocks to Henry's house. By the time I got there, some babies had already been born, but I got to see the rest of them come out, hairless and blind. *The miracle of bunny birth!* Henry and I had invested two dollars in the original male and female, and now we had ten babies. It was the kind of multiplication that really meant something to me. Dollar signs flashed before my eyes.

Riding home on my bike, it felt like flying. I was so excited until I saw my dad's pickup truck. He had come home earlier than expected from the pool hall, drunk as usual and now super mad. He made me break off a handful of switches from a tree and proceeded to beat the crap out of me, right there in the yard, in plain view of the neighbors.

Dad's reaction was typical, and it made no sense, but he was the king and we always had to do whatever he said. He was real big on me staying in the yard. In the summer between fifth and sixth grade, I was allowed to ride my bicycle on the sidewalk in front of the house, but no farther. When he was at work during the day, Mom allowed me a lot more discretion because she knew how controlling he was.

Once, when I was about ten years old, I rode my bike on a two-lane highway to Morganfield, seven miles away, to take my friend Zane to see his grandma. Zane, who was two years younger, sat behind me on the banana seat with his arms wrapped tightly around my torso as cars whizzed by. Of course, we were not wearing helmets. On the way home, my mom's best friend, Mary Nave, happened to drive by. She pulled over and rolled down the window.

"Ronnie Adams, what in the world are you doing out here on this road?" she asked, incredulous.

By the time I got home, Miss Nave had already ratted me out. Mom grounded me for two weeks, but she did not tell Dad because she knew he would probably beat me.

Most of the time, I would just ride all over town and pick up pop bottles other people had thrown in trash cans or on the ground. Back then, you could collect ten cents per bottle by returning them to a store, so they could be sent back to the bottling plant and reused. I loved saving up a couple of dollars now and then and buying little surprise gifts for my mom, like an ashtray or a flower vase. They only cost a dollar or two, but Mom always acted like they were wonderful, which made me feel good. Collecting pop bottles also made it possible to buy an occasional Coke and candy bar, and it was also how I made money to chip in on the rabbits. On the day the baby rabbits were born, maybe I shouldn't have violated Dad's rule about not leaving the house, but no kid deserves to be whipped for something like that.

As for the rabbits, Henry and I sold them and we made a little bit of money, but then we quit the business. We probably got bored; I don't remember. However, that was the first time I understood the concept of supply and demand and the beauty of capitalism.

I learned another valuable lesson about working hard and saving money at the local drugstore. One day, when I was ten, the store owner saw me staring at a Kodak 104 Instamatic camera, which was securely locked inside a glass display case.

"You like that?" he asked.

"Yeah, but I don't have enough money," I said.

"I'll tell you what," the man said, "I'll put it in a bag with your name on it, and whenever you come in, give me a dollar and I'll deduct it from what you owe."

The price was $19.95. I gave the man two dollars, and he wrote $17.95 on the bag. Every time I got a dollar from collecting pop bottles, I gave it to the drugstore owner. Soon, the camera was mine, and I used it all through grade school, junior high, and high school. It was a wonderful feeling, owning something that I had worked for.

4

Old-Time Religion

As much as I disdained my dad, I adored my mom. With Dad being an abusive drunkard, I could easily have become a juvenile delinquent, but Mom's unconditional love and support kept me on the straight and narrow. She always taught me to be kind to people. I learned the Golden Rule[3] from her before I even knew what it was called or that it came from the Bible.

Mom had chronic ulcers, which I'm sure resulted from all the fighting and the daily stress of struggling to make ends meet. She was also a smoker, which did not help matters. She was hospitalized maybe four or five times, for two or three weeks each time, during those early years. Whenever I was away from the house, even at school, I was afraid she would die before I could get home.

Mom was a believer, but nobody in our family went to church when I was a kid. Even then, I knew who Jesus was and I always had a feeling that he was on my shoulder. Once, I was terrified of going to Hell because I told someone to "shut up," which I thought was a cuss word.

Christmas was always strange. For one thing, there was never any talk of Jesus. Dad would get drunk and give me my presents two weeks early. As a kid, I didn't mind that, but then Christmas morning was always anticlimactic because there were no surprises. We did not usually have a Christmas tree, but one

---

3   "Do unto others as you would have them do unto you." - Luke 6:31 and Matthew 7:12

time we got a little two-foot shrub and stuck it in a coffee can with rocks in the bottom to hold it up. There were no lights, but we hung some ornaments on the shrub. It looked sort of like that scrawny little tree in *A Charlie Brown Christmas*. The best tree we ever had was when I was in the sixth grade. Mom saved up and bought one of those shiny, silver trees with a motorized wheel that turned and projected different colors on the branches. I remember sitting and watching it for what seemed like hours, mesmerized by the ever-changing colors on our magical, sparkling Christmas tree.

One day, a man was going up and down our street, selling big, white Bibles. When he came to our door, I wanted to buy one for the family, but the price was twenty dollars and I didn't have enough money. I convinced Mom that if she loaned me the money, I would pay it back over time by coming home for lunch instead of buying it at school. School lunches were twenty-five cents. I also got a job taking out the milk cartons in the cafeteria in exchange for free lunch. And, of course, I collected pop bottles and turned them in for the deposit. I never told Dad about that Bible, but Mom cherished it, even if she did not always read it. I still have it in my office.

In those early childhood years, church did not play much of a role in my life, so I am not sure what motivated me to buy that Bible. Somehow, I always just had a feeling God was a good thing and by doing good things for other people, I might balance some of the bad stuff in my life. Maybe it was Jesus speaking to me through my subconscious.

Before I bought that Bible, I had never read one. The only Bible verse I remember learning was Psalm 23 (*"The Lord is my shepherd; I shall not want…"*), which my Grandma Lucy taught me. She was Dad's mom. My maternal grandmother died when Mom was little.

My first church experience was with Jehovah's Witnesses when I was in the fourth grade. A Jehovah's Witness lady was going door to door, and Mom invited her in. The lady was so kind; she offered to drive my mom and me to the Jehovah's Witness Hall in Henderson, which was twenty-five miles away.

Every Sunday, she picked us up, drove us to her church, and brought us home. Dad never went.

I did not listen closely to what was being taught at the Jehovah's Witness Hall, but one thing that caught my attention in 1968 was a discussion about the end of the world. Of course, now I know the Bible teaches that nobody except God knows when the end will come, but at age eleven, I didn't know better. The Jehovah's Witnesses explained their beliefs during a big gathering one weekend. Somehow, they had figured out that the world was going to end in 1975. Instead of being scared, I remember being happy because Mom was very ill at that time. As often as she was sick, I was always worried that something would happen to her and I would be left alone with my dad. When I heard about the impending doomsday, I thought Mom could probably make it seven more years and then we could die together. It wasn't a morbid thought; it gave me a peaceful feeling, knowing there was something better than our miserable existence with Dad.

After I moved to Dawson Springs in the eighth grade, I started going to the First Baptist Church of Dawson Springs by myself. By that time, Mom worked on Sundays, so I walked to church and sat in one of the middle pews. Baptists have a reputation for being friendly, but I was pretty much on my own. Sunday after Sunday, I sat alone, and nobody befriended me. I went to that church until I graduated from high school. I finally stopped going because I became disillusioned with the other kids bragging about what they did on Saturday night and then showing up at church the next morning, acting holier-than-thou.

5

Hoop Dreams

There are few times in life when people have a true epiphany. Let me tell you about the precise moment when I knew, without a doubt, that my grand purpose was to be a professional basketball player. It happened when I was twelve.

I already loved the game, and I was getting to be pretty good by just playing with my friends in the backyard. One day, I tried out for the seventh-grade team and made it, even though I was in the sixth grade. I had previously played third string on the fifth-grade team at my school, but there was no budget for uniforms, so we just played in our street clothes. The seventh-grade team was the first one I was ever on, where we had real, honest-to-goodness jerseys. They were bright red. I was so proud of mine that I always pressed it before a game, taking care to iron out every wrinkle. I wanted to look my best on the court.

We made it to the semifinals that season. We were playing a tournament game and the score was tied, with four seconds left in the fourth quarter. During a timeout, our coach drew the play to tip the ball, which should have gone to our best player, but somehow it ended up in my hands. I was petrified, but there wasn't time to think about what was happening because the clock was about to run out, so with every bit of strength that I could muster, I gave it my best shot from outside the three-point line. As the ball sailed through the air, my stomach was in a knot. The ball went off to the side a little bit, and I thought I had missed the goal, but by some miracle, it banked in and we won the game! The buzzer buzzed, the crowd roared, and my teammates rushed me, slapping high-fives and patting me on the shoulder. I wasn't the best player on the team, but at that moment, I was a star.

We went out to eat afterward and my teammates' parents and other people must have bought me ten Cokes. My parents were not there; they never came to games, but it did not matter. I felt great. If I had not already been hyped-up from the adrenaline, the caffeine surely would have done it.

What I remember the most, though, was the bus ride home that night. Condensation trickled down the inside of my window as I gazed at eerie flames in the distance, where methane gas was burning off from oil wells and coal mines. It was almost hypnotic. I was just starting to relax when suddenly the silence was broken by the shouts of our cheerleaders sitting at the front of the bus: *"Rah rah for Ronnie! Rah rah for Ronnie! Someone's in the crowd, yelling rah rah for Ronnie! One, two, three, four—who you gonna root for? Rah rah for Ronnie, that's who!"*

I have often pondered whether people tend to become good at something because they like it, or if they like it because they are good at it. I don't know how it was with me, but I knew basketball was my life's calling right then and there. From then on, everyone treated me differently, even the teachers. My self-esteem shot up one thousand percent.

"I like this," I thought. *"This is good stuff."*

6

DAD'S DEMONS

Basketball was a form of escape from a home life that sucked. I wanted to love my dad, but I hated him. Everybody knew he was a tailhole. (That's a Kentucky word for another one that's not so polite.) He was mean, just for the sake of it.

When I was still on the fifth-grade team, the coach decided he would treat us by taking us to a high school game over in the next county. To us small-town kids who loved basketball, the prospect of going to a high school game was the coolest thing ever. It might as well have been the Boston Celtics as far as I was concerned. I already followed the regional high school players from stories in the *Louisville Courier-Journal* and *The Messenger* in Madisonville. I cut out their pictures and taped them to my bedroom wall.

When the big day arrived, Dad got drunk after work and decided I wasn't allowed to go to the game. I asked why, and he snapped, "Because I said so!" When the coach and my teammates pulled up at the house to pick me up, Dad made me give them the bad news. By the time one of my teammates, Ricky Harris, knocked on the door, I had just stopped crying. My eyes were red.

"Whatsa matter, Ronnie?" he asked.

"My dad says I can't go."

"How come?"

I tried to think of a sensible answer, but there wasn't one.

"I don't know," I said. "He just won't let me."

I started sobbing again.

"Dang," Ricky said.

Ricky was one of the black kids who used to play basketball with me in my backyard, so I think he already knew what my dad was like.

"Don't tell the other guys I was cryin', okay?" I asked.

"Okay, yeah."

"I hope y'all have fun," I said. "I'll see you at school."

I closed the door and peeked out the window as the coach's car pulled away with my teammates. The experience caused such a horrible feeling in the pit of my stomach. The game wasn't going to cost my dad anything and I hadn't done anything wrong to deserve a punishment, but he squelched my fun for no reason. It was so humiliating.

Another time, when we lived in a duplex, there was a family in the adjoining apartment with two children about my age who had bunk beds in their bedroom. Our living room closet abutted their bedroom. On many nights, Dad would get drunk, drag a big stereo console into the closet, shut the doors, and turn the volume up full-blast all night long just to be obnoxious. If the neighbors ever complained, I didn't know about it, but imagine how it felt having to ride the school bus with those kids the next day.

My dad was passive-aggressive. One minute, he could be in a good mood, but you never knew when he was going to suddenly turn on you, like a mad dog. Sometimes, when I was little, he would ask me to come over and sit by him and give him a hug. I reluctantly complied, even though I couldn't stand the acrid smell of alcohol on his breath. Other times, he would beckon me over to sit on his knee and sing him a song. One time, he asked me to sing Buck Owens' "Roll Out the Red Carpet." Why that one? I have no idea. Maybe he felt like he deserved to have a red carpet rolled out for him when he came home from work. He made me sing other songs, too, like Hank Williams' "Kaw-Liga," about a wooden Indian that's too afraid to tell a wooden Indian squaw how he feels about her: *"Poor ol' Kaw-Liga, he never got a kiss, Poor ol' Kaw-Liga, he don't know what he missed..."*

Yeah, I had to sing that for my dad. Now maybe you can understand why I hated that kind of music.

One night, while we were still living in Uniontown, Dad came in late, and he and Mom got into a big fight. At that time, we were living in a company-owned house, which was the best we had ever had. It was made of cinder blocks and had a concrete floor covered with tiles. I woke up in my bedroom to the sound of yelling from the living room and things breaking on the floor.

I was in the third grade, the first time I saw Dad hit Mom. He had her down on the floor, with his knees on her arms, and was punching her in the face. I was so scared I ran and hid under the bed. A few minutes later, I heard the screen door slam. Suddenly, everything was quiet. I stayed under the bed for what must have been twenty minutes, but it seemed like forever. I slid out from under the bed about the time Dad came back into the house. Mom was gone.

"Where's Mom?" I asked.

"They put her in jail," he mumbled.

I was confused. *Why is Mom in jail? You're the one who should be in jail, you S.O.B.!* (I didn't say that, but I thought it.)

The next day, I found out what had happened was this: After Dad attacked Mom, she went to the sheriff, but he did not want to fool with coming to the house to get me while Dad was drunk. (I know that doesn't make any sense, but we didn't live in Mayberry and our sheriff wasn't Andy Taylor.[4]) The sheriff had asked my mom if she thought Dad would hurt me, and she said no, so the sheriff decided to wait till morning to deal with things. Mom spent the night with a friend. She wasn't in jail; that's just what my dad told me. When the sheriff came to our house the next morning, Dad was no longer drunk and he had calmed down, so the sheriff didn't arrest him. I left with Mom and the sheriff, and we stayed with one of her friends for a couple of days until my oldest sister picked us up and took us to her home in Dawson Springs. Later, we reunited with Dad, as we did many times. The cycle repeated itself, as it often does with abusive relationships. I don't know why Mom never pressed charges.

---

4   Mayberry was the fictional town on the 1960s television series *The Andy Griffith Show*. Andy Griffith starred as the loveable Sheriff Andy Taylor.

The last time Dad threatened to attack Mom (that I was aware of) was when I was seventeen. He was always saying ugly things and she was at the point where she dished it back at him. I don't know how this confrontation started, but it was getting nasty.

"I'm gonna knock the hell out of you!" he yelled at Mom.

"No, you're not!" I said as I jumped in between them.

"Get out of the way, or you'll get it, too!" he shouted.

Despite his tough talk, Dad was trembling. He was 5'10" and weighed 180 pounds. I was 6'2" and 220 pounds. He wanted to hit me, but he knew that I would hit him harder, and he was scared. He snorted like a drunken horse with whiskey on its breath as we glared at each other. My heart pounded. I had never spoken that way to my dad. The standoff lasted about a minute until he gave up and stomped off to another room.

With so much volatility at home, sometimes it felt like things were okay, so long as there was no punching.

A rare, "happy" moment with mom and dad, celebrating Ron's 12th birthday.

7

Boys Will Be Boys

In Dawson Springs, we lived in a duplex, which we rented for $25 a month, just Mom and me. It was 1969. She made $1.62 an hour washing dishes in a nursing home. We painted the walls together. I liked living there because things were peaceful and it felt like a normal home. Then, about a year later, Dad came down from Uniontown and moved in with us. I was surprised Mom let him, but this time she had the power because it was her apartment; Dad's name wasn't on the lease. Overall, he behaved, but still drank heavily and spent more time at the pool hall than at home.

I attended Dawson Springs High School, which was small, even by small-town standards, with about 200 students. One of the most famous alums is former Kentucky Governor Steve Beshear, who was elected in 2007 and 2011. (His son, Andy, was elected governor in 2019.) However, Steve was ten years ahead of me. I did not know him, although the Beshear family was, and still is prominent in the area, and even has a local lake named after them.

Another prominent person who graduated from Dawson Springs High School is Scott Jennings, a writer and conservative political commentator best known for his many appearances on CNN and previously on Fox News. Scott graduated from Dawson Springs in 1996, twenty-one years after me. His father, Jeff "Tank" Jennings, and I were teammates on the Dawson Springs Panthers basketball team during my senior year and his junior year. Jeff later married another classmate of ours, Kelly Fassold, a friend of my niece, Beth.

I played baseball and ran a little track in high school, but basketball was what I loved most. High school basketball has always been a big deal in Kentucky, especially in small towns, where there isn't much to do on a Friday night. Many of our games sold out. As a poor kid from the wrong side of the tracks, who wore old clothes, I would not have stood much of a chance socially, but being a Panther won me a lot of friends and even a couple of girlfriends during the three years that I started varsity on the team.

The Dawson Springs Panthers, 1973-74. Back row, left to right: Joe Keller, Scott Summers, Chris Smiley, Charles Ramsey. Second row from left: Neal Shipp, Sammy Williams, Kenny Smith, Tim Wallace, Jeff Jennings. Front, from left: Coach Norman Manasco, Ron Adams, Jeff Eli, Billy Chappel. (Courtesy of The Messenger, Madisonville, Kentucky)

During my final two seasons with Dawson Springs, we won forty games, which was more than the Panthers had won in ten years. I was one of five starting players in my junior year, along with Kenny Smith, Scott Summers, Billy Chappel, and Jeff Eli—a true "iron-man five." Kenny and I were good friends, which led us to become fierce rivals, both on and off the court. We were always trying to outdo each other, though our personal competition never got in the way of our loyalty to the team.

Our coach, Norman Manasco, was nicknamed "Stormin' Norman" for good reason—he was tougher than a Marine drill sergeant. Sometimes, he reminded me of Bobby Knight, the legendary Indiana University coach notorious for throwing chairs and yelling at referees. Coach Manasco never did that as far as I knew, but to say he was intense would be an understatement. During my sophomore year, three seniors quit the Panthers because of ongoing clashes with him. One day I showed up at practice after lunch and was soon hunched over, sick at my stomach. "Stormin' Norman" went to his office and returned with a bottle of Pepto-Bismol tablets.

"Here, take a couple of these," he ordered. "Real winners play when they're sick."

I ate the tablets and limped back onto the court, trying to ignore the nausea. A minute later, my stomach felt like Mount Saint Helens[5] about to blow. I galloped as best I could, trying to avoid a premature eruption before I could get to the restroom on the second floor. I clenched my lips, but spurts of vomit trickled from my mouth, leaving a chunky trail of half-digested lunch and pink remnants of two chewed-up tablets in the hallway. Inside the men's room, I collapsed to the floor and finished throwing up into the drain. Just then, the coach came in.

"Don't come out till you're ready to play," he said, without any shred of sympathy.

It was a good thing I was too sick to speak because what I was thinking at that moment probably would have gotten me suspended. Five minutes later, I got up, wiped my face at the sink, and returned to the gym, fully intending to try to resume practice. However, one of my teammates, Jeff Eli, did something during a drill that caused Coach Manasco to yell at him. Jeff lost his temper and heaved the ball as hard as he could into the upper

---

5   A volcano in Washington State

bleachers. Furious, the coach blew his whistle and sent everyone home with an order to return at six o'clock the next morning to resume practicing for a big game that was scheduled that night.

I had dry heaves early in the evening before I drifted off. I felt a little better when I woke up at five a.m., but when I went to put on my jersey for practice, I realized I had left it on the porch. Ordinarily, I would have washed my jersey after practice, but I was so sick when I got home from school the day before that I had left it outside. Now it was frozen with icy sweat and puke. I grimaced as I slipped into the cold, slimy garment. After school, I got on the bus with the rest of the team and traveled one hundred miles to play the game. We lost, undoubtedly because I was still sick and the rest of the team was exhausted.

Still, we won about half our games. I set a school record during my sophomore year by scoring thirty-one points in one half of a game against Trigg County. Between my junior and senior years, I attended a basketball camp with one hundred-ten players at Murray State University, where I was voted most valuable player. In my senior year, I was named a member of the *Louisville Courier-Journal's* All-State High School Basketball Team, chosen by a board made up of coaches, sportswriters, and other officials from around the state. That season, I averaged over twenty-four points, nine rebounds, and nine assists per game. During my junior and senior seasons, we were 19-11 and 21-12. I was proud to be a Panther. There were a couple of times, however, when I came dangerously close to being kicked off the team because of sheer adolescent stupidity.

In September of my senior year, high school basketball

Ron Adams, ca. 1974
(source unknown)

coaches from around Kentucky gathered for a coaches' camp one weekend at Lake Barclay State Resort Park, about twenty miles from Dawson Springs. Even though the event was primarily for coaches, a few players were also expected to be there. Coach Manasco invited the Panthers to come along and sleep on the floor of his room at the park lodge. It sounded like fun, so off we went.

There were no formal competitions, but we played several pickup games—mostly three-on-three or five-on-five. I won a one-on-one competition against one of the best players in the state, which made me feel great.

Toward the end of the second day, as things were winding down, the coaches were hanging out at the swimming pool, socializing and drinking beers. My teammates and I were bored and had no interest in spending more time with adults, who probably did not want us eavesdropping on them anyway, so we decided to play a prank.

I don't remember who came up with this brilliant idea, but we filled our pockets with tiny pea gravel from the hotel's landscaping. On one side of the building, the roof extended almost to the ground, making it easy for us to get on it. We carefully climbed the steep slope to the apex, from which we could see the pool area on the other side, forty feet below. Taking careful aim, we started tossing pebbles, one at a time, occasionally striking some of the coaches on the top of the head or the back of the neck. They were already half-lit, which made their reaction so much funnier.

"What the shit was that?" one of them said.

The pebbles were too small to hurt anyone or to be seen coming through the air. The coaches smacked themselves as if they were being attacked by mosquitoes. We were laughing our butts off.

The sun had just set, and it was too dark for anyone to see us on the roof, but what we failed to realize was that people in the rooms below could hear our scuffling on the slate tiles. The next thing we knew, several park rangers were surrounding the lodge. My friends and I hid behind a chimney, but we were trapped like raccoons in a tree, with coonhounds sniffing us out from below. One of the rangers—an especially big, imposing man—climbed onto the roof, his flashlight in one hand and his gun in the other.

"All right, you guys, come out with your hands up!" he ordered.

Once we were back on the ground, the chief ranger lectured us.

"What in the hell were you boys doing on that slate roof?" he asked. "Don't you know you could slip and fall?"

My teammate Kenny, who was always so tough on the basketball court, was now reduced to tears.

"We didn't mean any harm," he blubbered. "You know how boys will be, sir."

You know how boys will be? I would have lost it if the situation had not been so serious.

"I've got a good mind to send you fellas to the Cadiz Hotel," the chief said.

Since we had not won a trip to a vacation resort on a TV game show, I assumed the "Cadiz Hotel" was the nearby jail. I had never committed a crime, but now I thought I would have a criminal record forever. Fortunately, the ranger let us go with a warning, but not before talking with Coach Manasco. As gruff as the coach could be, I was simultaneously heartened and ashamed to discover he had been bragging about us players to the other coaches that weekend, telling them what great boys we were and how we had such good values.

"I'm embarrassed at you guys," Manasco said. "You came here representing Dawson Springs and now look at you."

The hotel manager lectured us on how fragile and expensive slate tiles are. He said he would do a damage evaluation the next day and let us know if we owed any money. However, he never got back to us, so I assumed that we had caused no damage. The chief ranger let us go, and I was thankful my parents never found out about my involvement in the rooftop rock-throwing caper.

You would think we would have learned our lesson when it came to pranks, but about a month later, some of my teammates and I had another unpleasant run-in with the law. Halloween was approaching, and like everywhere else, folks in Dawson

Springs started putting pumpkins on their front porches. In our area, there was a tradition called "Guard of the Pumpkins," a game where groups of people would go around and try to steal or smash pumpkins while others guarded them. Some of my teammates and I were among the pumpkin marauders.

A new art teacher, "Mr. B.," had just started at our school and lived in a mobile home in Menser, a small community about five miles from Dawson Springs. One night, while he was out of town, some senior girls stood guard over a pumpkin in front of his trailer when my friends and I showed up to attack it. When the girls saw us coming, they grabbed the pumpkin and took it inside the trailer. I tried to push my way in, but the relatively thin door started to crack, so I backed off to avoid damaging it. As my friends and I turned to leave, Charles heaved a water balloon. Instead of hitting the exterior of the trailer, the balloon smashed through a plate glass window, causing a deafening crash. The girls screamed.

"Oh, no!" Charles said. "I swear I didn't mean to do that!"

Charles told the girls he was sorry. We dreaded having to apologize to Mr. B.

The next morning, in school, the principal called our names over the P.A. system and summoned us to the office. Coach Manasco was there, along with the sheriff.

"Were you boys over at the trailer park in Menser last night?" the sheriff asked.

"I'm the one who broke the window, but it was an accident," Charles admitted. "I'll pay for it."

"It's not just the window," the sheriff said. "There's other damage. Five thousand dollars' worth."

There was a collective gulp as my friends and I looked at each other, wondering if we were going to be wrongly accused of something we did not do.

As we discovered, there had been previous acts of vandalism at that trailer, and nobody knew who did it. Since the neighbors had seen me and my friends leaving right after hearing the window break, the sheriff assumed we were responsible.

"I have a good mind to expel you all," the principal said.

The timing could not have been worse. The first basketball game of the season was coming up soon against Bremen High School in neighboring Muhlenberg County. If we were expelled, we would not be allowed to play. Jeff Jennings and other Panthers could play since they were not involved in the trailer park incident. Jeff was one of our best players, but without the rest of us, Dawson Springs probably would not stand a chance.

"If you expel them, I'll quit," Coach Manasco told the principal.

After questioning a few more people at the trailer park later that day, the sheriff determined we were not involved in the previous damage. He did not arrest us, we did not get expelled, and the Panthers defeated Bremen by a score of 98-68 in the season opener. But two near-arrests within a few weeks taught me an important lesson: If something bad happens and you are in the middle of it, people will assume that you are guilty by association. I also learned that as mean as I used to think Coach Manasco was, he genuinely cared about his players.

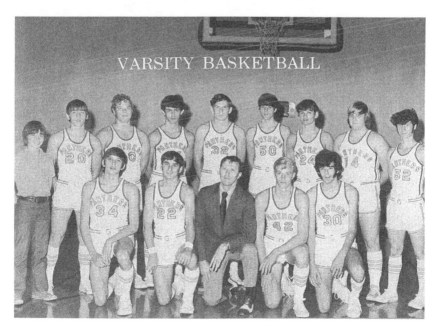

The Dawson Springs Panthers, 1973. Ron Adams is in the top row, third from right.
Coach "Stormin'" Norman Manasco is front-center.
(Courtesy of Dawson Springs High School)

Ron Adams (far left) in a game against the Earlington Yellow Jackets in January, 1973.
Also shown: Bill Lansden (with ball) and David Stone.
(Courtesy of The Messenger, Madisonville, Kentucky)

8

COLLEGE-BOUND

By my senior year, I was ranked third-best player in the region and best in the district and was starting to get noticed by some colleges. I signed a national letter of intent with James A. Faulkner State Community College in Alabama, which offered me an athletic scholarship. However, when Cumberland College made a similar offer, I jumped at the opportunity. The head coach at Faulkner was not pleased, but the letter of intent I had signed was not legally binding.

Cumberland College (now called the University of the Cumberlands) was in Williamsburg, Kentucky, about 250 miles east of Dawson Springs and closer to home than Faulkner State. More importantly, playing basketball at Cumberland meant I would get to play some games against the freshmen team of the NCAA champion Kentucky Wildcats at the University of Kentucky. I figured the coaches at UK would notice me and make me an offer. My goal was to eventually play for the Wildcats, which, in turn, would get me noticed by the NBA. At least, that was my strategy.

At Cumberland, I spent eight hours a day exercising, running, and practicing. Basketball was Job #1; studying was a distant second. I did not start off well academically, but as far as I was concerned, that was okay because I did not plan to get a degree, anyway. I was going to play college basketball long enough to make it to the NBA.

During a pick-up game one day in September—the second month of my freshman year— one of the guys undercut me and I came down hard on the side of my right ankle. The pain was sharp and intense as I hit the floor. For some reason, no one was available to take me to the hospital, so I was on my own as I limped to the car to drive myself thirty miles to the town of Corbin. To add insult to injury, when I got to the car, I saw that someone had broken into it and stolen the radio-tape cassette player that Mom gave me for high school graduation. All the tapes were gone, too. I wasn't sure which hurt worse—my ankle or my ego. I didn't care so much about the broken window, but that radio meant just about more to me than anything else because I knew how much Mom had to sacrifice to save up for it.

By the time I got to the hospital, my ankle had swelled up to the size of a football. The good news was there were no broken bones. The bad news was I had stretched some tendons and would be out for the season, which had not even started. The doctor drew fluid out of the swollen area so he could put a cast on my leg.

I could have stayed and finished my classes that first year, but I had no interest in living on a college campus without playing basketball. Since my right leg was in a cast, I used my left foot to control the gas and brake pedals while driving home to Dawson Springs. That might not have been the safest way to drive, but I did not think about it at the time. I had always been self-sufficient and did not want to ask someone else to help.

The next day, I went to see a doctor. That's where I met Robin, the receptionist, who was about a year and a half older than me and narcotically beautiful. When I laid eyes on her, all the pain in my foot disappeared. She already knew who I was because my basketball success in high school had made me something of a local celebrity. After some flirting, I asked her out and for the next few months, we were quite an item. We developed a very intimate relationship, but I had a feeling it was not going to work out in the long run. She was already talking about getting married and settling down, but I was intent on playing professional basketball. Still, we continued dating.

As soon as the cast came off in November, Dad made me an offer that I could not refuse. I mean, I literally could not refuse it, or there would have been trouble.

"Long as you're home, I got you a job at the mine; eight dollars an hour," he said. "You start at seven o'clock tomorrow morning."

I had not asked Dad to get me a job, and he did not ask if I wanted one. If he had asked me, I would have declined, but now that he had talked to his boss about hiring me, I could not turn him down, or there would be hell to pay. At least eight dollars an hour was good pay in 1975, compared to the minimum wage of two dollars, ten cents. I would be able to save money to go back to college. Even though I had a scholarship, it didn't cover everything.

"That's great, Dad," I said with feigned enthusiasm. "Thanks a lot!"

I doubt if Dad got me the job out of any sense of fatherly love. Or maybe it *was* his awkward way of showing love. I think he wanted to make sure that I wasn't just slacking around, doing nothing. When I was still in high school, Mom mentioned to him I would often go riding around with an older kid, who was a basketball player and a bit more rambunctious than me. Dad got worried that the older teenager was going to corrupt me and get me drunk. What he did not realize was that his own drinking had already convinced me to stay away from alcohol. Sure, I would open beer cans for my friend, but I did not drink. I was afraid that I might like it, and I did not want to take the risk of getting hooked.

For the remainder of 1975 and throughout 1976, I learned how to be a coal miner. I carpooled sixty miles to work in Uniontown each day in a smoky car, with men with dirty mouths, only to spend ten hours in a dirty mine with other men whose dreams had long ago vanished. What kept me from sinking into depression was the hope that, soon, I would be out of the mine and back on the basketball court, in front of cheering crowds and adoring fans, on the fast track to a multimillion-dollar NBA contract.

My hoop dreams began to fade when I realized that both Cumberland and Faulkner had lost interest in me. When I left Cumberland after injuring my ankle, I told the coach I would not come back. After spending a couple of months there, I realized I did not like the desolate feel of the campus on weekends. As far as Faulkner was concerned, I was basically "persona non grata" after reneging on the letter of intent I had signed the previous year. Having been out of the spotlight for almost a year, I had lost my momentum, gained a few pounds, and burned bridges with the only two colleges that were previously interested in me. It no longer mattered I was once a high school basketball star in rural Kentucky. Fame is fleeting.

With no immediate basketball prospects, I continued working in the coal mine until I could figure out my next step. One day, early in 1977, I got together with Lolo to get her advice. Now thirty-nine years old, she was my sister, a trusted friend, and a mother figure all in one. She was one of the few people with whom I could discuss anything.

"It looks like I'm not going to be able to play basketball, but I don't want to work in the mine," I said.

"Well, then, you should do something different," she replied. "Have you thought about mine management?"

The local community college had a mining program, and the coal company offered tuition reimbursement. With the right education, I could get a job as a mine superintendent, where most of the work would be aboveground and the money would be great. I decided to look into it and maybe start the program in the fall. Meanwhile, I would stick with my present job and keep saving money.

A few days later, one of my fellow miners, who was about my age, invited me to drive with him to Louisville the next day to see a big high school basketball playoff game. Taylor County was playing Ballard County in the Kentucky State High School Basketball Tournament, and he had an extra ticket.

"Oh, man, I wish I could, but I'm scheduled to work," I said.

"Just call in sick; that's what I'm doing," he said. "They'll get someone to fill in for you."

I must admit I gave it serious thought, but just for a minute. I never liked to take advantage of people and I would not have felt right about lying to my boss just to go to a basketball game.

"Thanks for the offer, but I'll skip it this time," I said. "Have fun."

The next day, I got up dark and early as usual for the hour-long ride with people I didn't like, to a job I didn't like, thanks to a father I wished I could like. I clocked in and climbed into the cart that would carry me and ten other guys deep into the mine.

That was March 17, 1977, the last day that I would ever set foot underground.

9

BROKEN NECK,
SHATTERED DREAMS

Evansville, Indiana was across the Ohio River and just a few miles away, but the ambulance took me to Hopkins County Hospital in Madisonville, Kentucky, about an hour south of the mine, closer to my home in Dawson Springs. I must have been unconscious because I don't remember the ride.

I woke up in the ER, realizing someone was cutting off my pants, but it was weird I could not feel my legs. Confused thoughts flooded my mind as someone wheeled me to an X-ray machine. I could not move voluntarily, but my body was trembling from shock. A few minutes later, I overheard doctors and nurses talking to each other, and one of them said, "His neck is broken." I started to cry. I did not know much about physiology and anatomy, but I knew that people die from broken necks in car wrecks all the time, so I realized my condition was not good.

After rolling me to another room, someone said they were going to drill holes in my skull and put screws in to hold my neck in place, which really freaked me out. They must have given me more sedatives because I began to relax as I lay there for another fifteen or twenty minutes. I assumed they would use some kind of high-tech medical device, but when the doctor came back in, he was holding a power drill that looked like something you might find in an old tool shed.

A nurse cleaned my forehead, near where the hairline recedes on each side. I am sure she numbed it because I did not feel any pain, but I was wide awake during the beginning of the procedure. I could hear the high-pitched whirring of the drill right next to my ear. It was worse than any drill at a dentist's office. When they told me they were just going to bore a small hole in my skull, I thought about how many times I had seen a drill go too far through a piece of wood. I wondered, *Should I tell them to be careful, because the drill could punch through and go into my brain?*

The knockout drug must have kicked in because I don't remember when they finished the first hole, much less the second, third, and fourth. Following the surgery, I drifted in and out of consciousness, waking up occasionally, vaguely sensing different people were coming into the room. My half-sister,

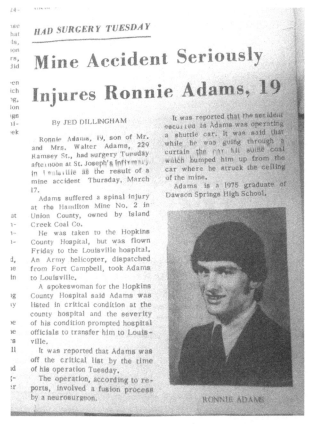

HAD SURGERY TUESDAY

Mine Accident Seriously Injures Ronnie Adams, 19

By JED DILLINGHAM

Ronnie Adams, 19, son of Mr. and Mrs. Walter Adams, 229 Ramsey St., had surgery Tuesday afternoon at St. Joseph's Infirmary in Louisville as the result of a mine accident Thursday, March 17.

Adams suffered a spinal injury at the Hamilton Mine No. 2 in Union County, owned by Island Creek Coal Co.

He was taken to the Hopkins County Hospital, but was flown Friday to the Louisville hospital. An Army helicopter, dispatched from Fort Campbell, took Adams to Louisville.

A spokeswoman for the Hopkins County Hospital said Adams was listed in critical condition at the county hospital and the severity of his condition prompted hospital officials to transfer him to Louisville.

It was reported that Adams was off the critical list by the time of his operation Tuesday.

The operation, according to reports, involved a fusion process by a neurosurgeon.

It was reported that the accident occurred as Adams was operating a shuttle car. It was said that while he was going through a curtain the car hit some coal which bumped him up from the car where he struck the ceiling of the mine.

Adams is a 1975 graduate of Dawson Springs High School.

RONNIE ADAMS

Courtesy of Dawson Springs Progress

Sherry, and her minister-husband, Roger, who lived in Bristol, Tennessee, were present, which I thought was a bad sign. *Don't relatives come from far away when a patient is about to die?* I also noticed it stormed that first night.

When I fully awoke twenty-four hours later, I still had not talked with a doctor, but Mom confirmed what I already knew—my neck was broken. She said the doctors had scheduled me for another surgical procedure but canceled it twice because they were trying to decide if they could adequately care for me at that hospital. Five hours later, they determined I would need to be treated at the now-defunct St. Joseph's Infirmary in Louisville, 150 miles away. I still had not had a conversation with a doctor about my condition. I guess there was no good news, so the doctors did not want to say anything. I was terrified, not knowing the long-term implications of a broken neck.

An Army helicopter flew up from Fort Campbell, fifty miles south of Madisonville. As the staff lifted me onto a different gurney to load me into the helicopter, I felt a sudden, intense pain in my neck. I don't know if they lifted me the wrong way or if the pain was normal, but it subsided after they laid me back down.

Mom rode in the chopper with me. The crew taped two pillows over my ears to muffle the roar of the motor. They must have given me another sedative because I don't remember much about the flight until we arrived in Louisville. I thought about the high school basketball game in Louisville the day before—the one that my friend had invited me to—the one that I skipped. *"If only I had lied to my boss, I wouldn't be in this situation now!"* I thought. As the ambulance left the airport, we almost collided with another vehicle on the way to the hospital. I could not see what happened, but I felt the ambulance lurch and heard people yell. Luckily, there was no accident.

At St. Joseph's, they put me on a Stryker frame, a bed that is designed to secure a patient in such a way he can be rotated without having to be lifted from the mattress. Weights are adjusted to keep everything balanced, but something broke as they were turning me and I fell halfway out before one of the aides caught me. After the near-accident in the ambulance and falling out of bed in the hospital, I wondered if I would survive long enough for an operation.

The surgical procedure in Madisonville was a temporary fix. In Louisville, the doctors did a spinal fusion, which involved taking a bone chip from my hip and putting it in my neck, with screws and pins to stabilize it. Then they put a neck collar on me and ordered me to lie flat for six weeks.

The whole time I worked in the coal mine, I never felt as claustrophobic as I did in that hospital bed with a contraption around my neck, unable to move. The only thing that made the monotonous hours of immobility bearable were the visitors, of which there were many—high school friends, Coach Manasco, my mom, sisters and their husbands. And, of course, my sweetheart, Robin. Dad never came. I am not sure why, but I assumed he was not handling it well. The only person from the coal mine who came to see me was my boss, who had ordered me to drive the shuttle car on the day of my accident. He was from India. His English was not great, but he was extremely apologetic. Oddly, I never felt any resentment toward him. Accidents happen and I did not blame him for mine.

Since I had partial use of my arms, I was able to hold a fork to feed myself, but I had to be careful because the least little thing could cause me to lose control and jab the roof of my mouth, often causing it to bleed. One day, one of my former Panthers teammates, Kenny Smith, came to visit with some other friends. He and I had been fierce competitors for so long, but now he saw me completely helpless, barely able to raise my arms. I am not sure who felt more awkward.

"I'm so sorry you're going through this," Kenny said as he held the fork up to my mouth, one bite at a time.

Mom and my sister Joyce got a hotel room nearby. Mom sat with me during the day and Joyce stayed with me at night. Joyce was funny, and she kept me laughing.

"Do you know my nose itches?" I asked her once, in the middle of the night.

"No, but if you hum a few bars, maybe we can sing it," she answered.

That tickled me, and we both laughed and laughed—me, for the first time since before the accident. It was so spontaneous.

After that, I started having her bring tapes into the room and play music. One of our favorites was the soundtrack recording of the Barbra Streisand and Kris Kristofferson movie *A Star is Born*. I especially loved the theme song "Evergreen" (*"Love soft as an easy chair..."*). Sometimes Joyce would sing, sometimes I would sing, and sometimes we sang together. We kept the volume low to avoid disturbing other patients, but soon we discovered the nurses were listening to us over the intercom at the nurses' station down the hall. They found our late-night duets very entertaining. Thanks to Joyce, I was starting to feel alive again.

Meanwhile, the doctors never told me anything specific about my diagnosis or prognosis. I think they were primarily concerned with keeping me alive and stabilizing my functions. I was getting fevers of about 103 degrees every day for about ten days. The doctors gave me Tylenol and put ice on me. After a few days, they put me on an ice mattress. I could not feel the cold, except high up on my shoulders.

During the month or so that I was at St. Joseph's, I dropped from 202 pounds to 148 and my waist shrank from 34 to 29 inches. I went from wearing an extra-large shirt to a small. If I could have figured out how to put such rapid weight loss into a diet pill, I would have made a fortune.

Following my discharge, I was sent straight over to The Rehabilitation Center, not far from St. Joseph's. When I first arrived, they put me in a reclining wheelchair, which allowed me to sit up for the first time in the thirty days since my accident.

Now known as Frazier Rehab Institute,[6] The Rehabilitation Center was, and still is, considered a world-class acute rehab facility, but the doctor in charge of my case could have used some lessons in bedside manner. He rolled me outside and

---

6   "History of Frazier Rehab Institute," www.uoflhealthnetwork.org, Frazier Rehabilitation Institute, Access Date April 3, 2021, https://www.uoflhealthnetwork.org/frazier-rehab-institute-more-about-frazier

immediately started telling me all the bad news about how serious my condition was and all the things I would never be able to do, including walk, which was the first time I had heard that. He just seemed to be checking off a laundry list of things that he probably told all patients. He even warned me that if I were to visit another country, the impurities in the water would probably kill me. *"Why are you telling me this NOW?"* I thought. *"Does it look like I'm planning to drive to the airport and fly to Mexico?"*

He went on telling me about how people with my type of injury die predominantly from urinary and bladder infections and pressure sores and other similarly nasty things. He was immediately negative and impersonal, so I tuned him out.

When Dr. Doom finished handing down my life sentence, an aide rolled me back to my room. I laid there and cried for four or five hours as it grew dark outside. *"Is this how it ends?"* I wondered. Visitors were not allowed at The Rehabilitation Center, so that night was the first time I was completely alone in my room, without my mom or sister.

Crying alone is a strange thing. What is the point if no one sees you doing it and shows some sympathy for your pain? It's sort of like the old philosophical question, *If a tree falls in the middle of a forest and there is no one there to hear it, does it make a noise?*

When I woke up the next morning, my face hurt from all the crying the night before. I realized that before I cried, I could not walk, and now that I had cried all night, I still could not walk and *now my face hurts*! That is when I understood that tears were just a waste of time. That's not quite true, of course. Crying does have psychological and even physiological benefits, but right then and there, I decided that if an action did not cause a positive response, I would not do it. From then on, I would approach life as a basketball game—*What do I have to play with and how am I going to use the resources currently at my disposal?*

During those first few weeks following my accident, I was extremely weak. One of the first physical things the therapist had me do was to push myself in a wheelchair from my room to the cafeteria. The wheels had "quad pegs" attached to the rims; rubber-coated handles that allowed patients, like me, who could not grip the rim to push forward. Even though the cafeteria was just 250 feet down the hall, it took thirty minutes to get there the first time I did it by myself. After seeing me struggle, my mother told my sister Lolo that I looked like "a little broken bird." Mom never said that directly to me, but Lolo told me about it much later.

I could see the pain in my mother's face every time she came to visit. The first day the occupational therapist was teaching me to put my pants on, I struggled for thirty minutes just to get the pant legs up to my knees. Mom was watching but left the room in tears. My sisters told me they and Mom had a rule that nobody was allowed to cry in front of me. I did not feel as bad for myself as much as I did for my mother, just knowing how much my situation was hurting her. I felt useless, but Lolo gave me a pep talk.

"You've never given up on anything before, have you?" she asked.

"No," I answered.

"Well, don't give up now! You have to keep going!"

One of the more embarrassing aspects of rehab was dealing with catheterization. Most of the time, I used a Texas catheter, a condom-like device that fit over my penis so that I could urinate any time and the urine would go through a tube into a plastic bag. However, four times a day, a nurse had to do a regular catheterization, which involved sticking a tube all the way up my penis to drain my bladder completely. One day, a group of young student nurses were making rounds, and the regular RN asked me if they could observe the catheterization procedure. I reluctantly agreed. Within seconds, I had an erection as several cute, young women my age stood there, watching. Of course, it was involuntary; I could not control it. Thankfully, there was no giggling; the student nurses were very professional and respectful. I just closed my eyes and waited for it to be over.

Most of the other patients at The Rehabilitation Center were a lot older than me, and some could not speak. We had little in common. Maybe I was being selfish at that time, but I did not want to hang out with them. Except for my physical therapy sessions, I spent a lot of time alone. During this period, I began to reflect more on God and life and where I would go from here.

I started getting audiocassette tapes of the Bible. At first, somebody borrowed them from a library, but then someone else bought a few for me. The ones from the library were the King James version. The other ones were the Revised Standard Edition (RSE), which is in more contemporary language and easier to understand. The RSE tapes were read by actor Alexander Scourby, whose best-known film role was that of the tough mobster Mike Lagana in the classic 1953 film noir movie *The Big Heat*, but on the Bible tapes he had a deep, soothing voice. I thought *"That's what Jesus sounds like!"* I would listen to those tapes over and over, especially the Gospel of Matthew, chapter four—the story of when Jesus spent forty days and nights in the desert and was tempted by Satan, and Jesus said, "Get behind me, Satan." I must have listened to that story 200 times. It was so powerful and made me feel closer to Jesus than ever.

During my off time at The Rehabilitation Center, listening to the Bible tapes was the most important thing for me. It was very comforting, hearing Alexander Scourby read, *"Come to me, all who labor and are heavy laden, and I will give you rest."* Another of my favorite verses was, *"I am the resurrection and the life. Whoever believes in me, though he die, yet shall he live."* None of that was new. I had been hearing Bible verses every Sunday for the past few years at the First Baptist Church of Dawson Springs. But sometimes, old things take on a whole new meaning when circumstances change, and mine sure had. For the first time, I truly understood I was completely and utterly helpless, but Jesus was there to comfort me.

There were many lonely moments at The Rehabilitation Center. Visitors were allowed just a couple of hours in the evening, so it was comforting whenever a staff member came in. However, there was one person who took some getting used to. One of the orderlies was a gay gentleman, who I guessed to be in his late forties. Each night, after getting me ready for bed, he would brush my hair back and kiss me on the forehead. He never made an overtly sexual move. I am sure he just cared about me as a patient, but the forehead kisses made me uncomfortable. Was it because the orderly was gay, or because I had never been kissed by another guy, including my dad, and his affectionate gesture dredged up painful memories of a father who did not care enough to visit me in my darkest moments? I don't know the answer to that question, but I got used to the orderly's forehead kisses and never complained.

In most hospitals, a patient can call for help by pushing a call button on the bed, but at The Rehabilitation Center, there was a "call ball" hanging from a string, which I could hit with my hand and cause a bell to ring. One night, when I was alone, the call ball had been moved just slightly out of my reach. I was extremely thirsty and there was a glass of water on a table two feet away. I lay there for two or three hours, staring at that glass, unable to get anyone's attention. It was a reminder of how reliant I now was on other people and how I would need to learn to be patient and not panic when things did not immediately go the way they should.

Even in the darkest, loneliest moments in rehab, I never questioned my faith. I sensed such a closeness to Jesus. I thought of him as a superhero. Listening to Alexander Scourby reading the New Testament on tape made everything feel so real, like when the Pharisees tried to trip Jesus up with religious technicalities. He always had the right words for any situation, and he did miraculous things, but never in a flashy way. My mom had always taught me to treat everyone with respect and never act as if I was better than anyone else, but hearing the stories of Jesus setting those kinds of examples made the lessons so much more relevant.

Everything was a struggle, even the simplest of tasks, but some were more fun than others. I especially enjoyed an art project that was intended to strengthen my hand-eye coordination. The therapist placed a thin copper sheet, about eight by eleven inches, over a wood-engraving of Leonardo da Vinci's "The Last Supper." A brace was attached to my right hand to allow me to hold a stylus between my thumb and fingers, like a pencil. Each day, for twenty days, I spent an hour slowly rubbing the stylus over the copper sheet, which caused the image of "The Last Supper" to come through. I could hardly raise my hand; all I could do was move it back and forth a little bit, with my elbow resting on the table, but when it was finished, I had a beautiful, embossed image of Jesus and the Disciples, suitable for framing.

I started asking people to write scriptures about healing on pieces of paper and tape them to the wall in my room. One of the hospital workers, a young Christian woman, wrote John 3:16 *("For God so loved the world…")* and John 10:10 *("I have come that they may have life, and that they may have it more abundantly.")* Some of the doctors thought I was crazy. They never actually said that, but it was obvious. One of them, who I will call Dr. Doubt, would say things like, "You can't just sit around and wait for God to heal you." It was true that I did not believe my condition would be permanent, but I never told anyone I was going to just sit around, waiting for a miracle. That was his knee-jerk reaction to my faith.

After a while, I was sent to see a staff psychiatrist. I expected him to treat me as if I were insane, but he was very respectful. We talked for about two or three hours, and although he did not say it, I learned later he thought I could go to law school. It was one of the comments he wrote in my file.

When one of the physical therapists mentioned what the psychiatrist had written, my first thought was, *"Are you kidding?"* Before the accident, my goal had been to play professional basketball or, if I did not make it to the NBA, to maybe teach PE at a high school. I figured I didn't have to be super smart to do that, and I wouldn't have to spend so much time reading and studying. (My apologies to PE teachers, who really are smart. Please remember—I was young and naïve.)

If some of the doctors thought I was crazy for believing in God, I thought they were even crazier to think that I could be a lawyer. Forget the fact that I had been an average student in a small-town high school in rural Kentucky. How could I possibly go to college when I could not even go to the bathroom? If, by some miracle, I could get into law school and pass the bar, who would hire me? I could not hold a telephone, so how could I take calls from clients? How could I type legal documents and get from one courthouse to another? What judge or jury would take me seriously? As a basketball player, I was as tall as most of my teammates and opponents, but how persuasive could I be, sitting in a wheelchair in a courtroom, with opposing counsel towering above me, pacing back and forth and making dramatic gestures with his arms during closing arguments? (Isn't that how they all do it? I had seen them in movies and on TV.) All I could think about, at that moment, was "how" and "can't" and "no way" and "impossible."

Still, if a psychiatrist thought that I had the qualities needed to succeed in the legal profession, maybe I should listen. After contemplating the doctor's seemingly preposterous suggestion, I uttered one of the most powerful words in the English language: "Huh." Not with a question mark, the way people say it when they did not hear something. Not with an exclamation point, the way people say it when they are disgusted. Just with a period, in a neutral tone of voice, as if to imply, "Maybe."

When you think about it, "Huh" has probably preceded some of the greatest advancements in human history. I can imagine Thomas Edison saying "Huh" the first time he figured out how to make a practical light bulb. Henry Ford might have said it when he realized how an assembly line could be used to mass-produce an affordable automobile. Orville and Wilbur Wright probably said it when they discovered that by bending a wing slightly, they could control the direction of their flying machine.

Just like a house, great achievements are made of bricks, each one an idea. Each brick is a "Huh" moment. When somebody said they thought I could be a lawyer, my initial reaction was to close the door on the suggestion, but just before it slammed shut, I thought, "Huh." I decided to leave the door open. I was not buying into the idea right away, but I started to at least think that *maybe* it could be accomplished.

Jesus cracked the door for everyone, including me. Maybe it was time to see what was on the other side.

10

HOME IS WHERE
THE HEARTBREAK IS

Quadriplegia is the most physically traumatic condition that a person can survive with for decades. There are other debilitating conditions, like multiple sclerosis (MS), Lou Gehrig's disease, and others, but people who have them generally do not live long. Since World War II, many advances have been made in the treatment of spinal cord injuries (SCI), and now quadriplegics can live a long time.

There are different degrees of quadriplegia; the severity depends on the cause of the condition and the exact location of the spinal injury. My spinal cord was injured between the C5 and C6 vertebrae near the base of my neck. Some quadriplegics have zero use of their arms or legs, while others have limited mobility. I have partial use of my arms, but my hands do not function. My fingers are curled into clenched fists as if I am getting ready to punch someone. Some quadriplegics need a ventilator to help them breathe. I do not. Some are unable to speak. I can talk (although I can think of a few people who probably wish I would not).

Since my accident had occurred as a result of my boss telling me to operate a piece of machinery for which I was not trained, you might think the company was liable and could be sued for millions of dollars, but that was not the case. I went to see a lawyer, David Massamore, who had handled both my dad's and my uncle's black lung claims against the coal company. He explained that since my accident was work-related, I was only entitled to receive a grand total of $104 per week from Workers' Comp for the rest of my life, with no cost-of-living increase. However, the good news was that Workers' Comp would also cover my ongoing therapy and other medical needs, which otherwise would be cost-prohibitive for the average person. I was below average when it came to money.

I celebrated my twentieth birthday in rehab on April 26 and was discharged in mid-June, about three months after my accident. Though I was glad to be back home, I felt insecure. I spent the summer of 1977 getting used to my new normal. Those first few weeks back in Dawson Springs were like a roller coaster of emotions—one minute, high, the next minute, low. Despite being completely dependent on others for even the most personal functions, I was blessed to have caregivers who never acted as if I was a burden.

My sister, Joyce, and her husband, Howard, invited me to move into their home, where I could use my nephew's vacant room. He was four years older than me and had recently moved out. At first, it was a disaster because nothing was set up the way it needed to be. Howard built a temporary wheelchair ramp to the front door, but it was too steep. Also, the chair would not fit easily through the doors and there was hardly enough room to get it into position in the bedroom, so that I could transfer into the bed. The lack of space in my bedroom caused the catheter tube to bunch up and crimp, which resulted in urine backing up, which, in turn, caused the Texas catheter to slip off. My first day back home, my poor mom had to change the bed and me thirteen times. You can imagine how awkward it was for her to handle every intimate nook and cranny of my body. However, as she said, it was nothing that she had not seen before.

In addition to my mom and sisters, one comforting influence in my life during this period was Billy Deane, a distant cousin on my mom's side of the family. I did not know him well while growing up, even though we were the same age and lived in Dawson Springs. During high school, he worked a lot of jobs and I was busy with basketball, so we never socialized together. However, after I came home from Louisville, Billy suddenly became my best friend. One thing we spent a lot of time doing was playing chess.

Before I was injured, I never had much interest in sedentary games. I probably did not play chess more than ten or fifteen times, but it's amazing how your priorities change when you're confined to a bed or a wheelchair, with nothing else to preoccupy your time and your mind. Two or three times a week, Billy would come over and sit beside my bed and we would play chess for three or four hours. The board was on a little table next to the bed, and he would set up the pieces and make moves for me, as I directed. Now that I was not distracted by so many other things, I learned to focus more on the game and think strategically. About nine times out of ten, I was the one saying, "checkmate!"

Billy was so different from me in many ways. He had long hair and a beard and was less conservative, but he had such a kind heart. Even though we had not known each other well as teenagers, I think he felt empathy with me, seeing how I had lost so much because of the accident, and he wanted to help. I have always felt grateful for his kindness.

At six feet, two inches tall and two hundred-twenty pounds, Billy was strong enough to pick me up from my wheelchair and place me in the passenger seat of his pickup truck, which he did more times than I can remember. To lift me, he placed his arms under my arms and wrapped them around my back, with my arms wrapped around his shoulders. In that way, I hugged him as a friend. Sometimes we went to movies or hung out at his house. Other times, we just drove around.

One of the things young people did for fun in Dawson Springs was cruise around town to check out who else was cruising around. I loved riding around with Billy and seeing other old friends until one of them might look at me a certain way or say something that made me think they felt sorry for me. I sensed that many people who used to admire me as a basketball player now felt guilty talking to me, which made me feel worse.

It was especially awkward the first time I ran into my girlfriend, Robin when she was riding around with one of her girlfriends in a brand-new Datsun 280Z. It reminded me of how I had been planning to buy a Corvette before I got hurt, but now I couldn't.

One day, Robin came to break my heart. Or did I break hers? Maybe both. When I was first hospitalized in Louisville, she drove up every weekend to visit me. Then, it became every other weekend, and then every third. We were clearly drifting apart. I think she just did not know how to handle the situation. On that day, in my bedroom in my sister's home, the conversation was strained as we danced around the inevitable. Finally, I said what needed to be said.

"Look, Robin, we both know I'm not getting any better. I know you won't say it, so I will. Why don't we move on? You can see other people, and we can still be friends."

"Oh, Ronnie…"

And that was that. We cried as we hugged. It wasn't what I wanted, but it was necessary at that time.

Now that I was living in a home environment, one of the problems I had to deal with was frequent tearing of the skin just above my butt crack. If I wasn't careful, when I transferred from my chair to my bed, the process of sliding on the transfer board would pull my butt cheeks apart, stretching the skin and reopening a sore just over my tailbone. When that happened, I would have to stay in bed for several days to allow the sore to heal. It is a common problem for people who share my condition.

In the beginning, I needed to be turned every two hours during the night to avoid getting bedsores. The women in the family worked out a plan—Mom would turn me at midnight, just before I fell asleep. Joyce would get up and turn me at two o'clock in the morning. At 4:00 a.m., my sixteen-year-old niece, Lisa, would take a turn. At 6:00 a.m., Mom would get back up and do it again. None of us was getting enough sleep.

One of the good things about moving in with my sister was that her street was on a slight incline, which allowed me some much-needed exercise. The wheels on my chair had "quad pegs," rubber-coated handles that allow people who cannot grip the rim to move the chair by pulling on the pegs. Even though I could not grip the pegs, I could pull up on them with my wrists. Using that technique, I was able to roll myself up the street for about the length of a football field, which took about ten minutes, then I would coast back to the starting point and do it again. I built up my strength to where I could go up that hill four or five times in a row. However, I had to be especially careful about becoming overheated. Quadriplegics cannot sweat because the spinal cord is what tells your sweat glands when you are hot. My face, neck, and arms could feel when I was getting too hot, so I knew when to quit and go back inside, where it was air-conditioned.

Unfortunately, my sister's house could not easily be modified to accommodate my wheelchair, which meant getting around was more complicated than it needed to be. The insurance company found a twenty-five-year-old used double-wide mobile home at a dealership in Middlesboro, Tennessee. The windows were broken out and it needed a new furnace, but it would have to do for the time being. They moved it to the vacant lot next to my mom's trailer in Dawson Springs, and I moved in. Eventually, I had to reimburse the insurance company $5,000 for my "new" home.

11

ROCKY MOUNTAIN HIGH

The insurance agent in charge of my case was a man named Craig Riddell, and even though the coal company was his client, he went out of his way to help me. One day he called to tell me he had heard about a rehab facility called the Craig Hospital in Englewood, Colorado, a suburb of Denver, where they were supposedly having great success treating people with spinal cord injuries. He made it sound so amazing that I naturally wanted to try it.

It took a couple of months to process the paperwork and make travel arrangements for me and my wheelchair, but I finally flew to Denver in late October of 1977. It was my first time traveling more than 500 miles from home and my first time flying. Mom drove me to the airport in Nashville, Tennessee, ninety-nine miles from Dawson Springs. The plane was parked on the tarmac, away from the terminal. Passengers boarded the plane by walking up portable stairs, but for me, that was impossible. Instead, the crew put me on a food service forklift and got me onto the plane through the rear entrance. I felt like a piece of cargo, but once I was situated onboard, everything went smoothly. I enjoyed looking out the window at the puffy, white clouds and the ground far below during the two-and-a-half-hour flight.

The Craig Hospital was founded by Frank Craig in 1907 as the "Tent Colony of Brotherly Love" in Lakewood, Colorado, to treat indigent tuberculosis patients. Through the years, the tents were replaced by buildings and the name was changed to Craig Colony as the facility's reputation began spreading. Thanks to antibiotics, tuberculosis was largely under control by 1955, so Craig's focus shifted to the treatment of other medical conditions, including spinal cord injuries. Craig relocated to its present facility in 1970 and in 1975 became known as Craig Hospital.[7]

At the Denver airport, a hospital attendant helped me off the plane. I arrived at the Craig Hospital with all the stuff I thought I needed, including a big foam rubber pad to sleep on, with a hole cut for my hips to fit into. A nurse came in and said, "What's all that in the corner?" When I told her that I had brought it to sleep on, she said, "Naw, naw, naw, you don't need that. We're going to put you on sheepskin and we are going to check your skin tolerance. Within a month, you'll be able to lay for six hours before having to be turned. You don't rest well, being awakened every two hours." Believe me, that was as big a homerun as I had experienced since the injury! The previous rehab center had been giving me the wrong information about how to sleep. If Craig did not do anything other than that, it would have been a giant win, but I quickly learned there was much more about that place to like.

The Craig Hospital did everything different than I had experienced in Louisville. First of all, Craig was predominantly for brain and spinal cord injuries, whereas in Louisville, most of the other patients were stroke patients and they were much older. In Denver, there were at least fifty patients with spinal cord injuries and six with brain injuries. Many of the patients were close to my age and everybody's condition was similar to mine, so I could relate to them. I did not feel so self-conscious, watching other people struggle to do the same things that I was struggling to do. We were learning together. For the first time since my injury, I felt like I fit in.

The other improvement over the previous facility was the positive attitude overall. The morning after my arrival, I met with

---

7   "History of Craig Hospital," www.craighospital.org, The Craig Hospital Foundation, Access Date September 13, 2020, https://craighospital.org/about/history-of-craig

some doctors and told them, "I'll do anything you ask, as hard as I can, but don't tell me I can't do something." They said that's how they wanted it.

Right off the bat, the physician in charge of my case, Dr. Ward Curtis, was very supportive and it was great to work with him. He and his team got me into a regular routine, like in real life. They would wake me early in the morning, get me into the shower, dress and shave me, brush my teeth and such, before 8:00 a.m. Then came breakfast, always in the cafeteria, not my room. They treated me like every other person there.

One of the first things I did each day, after breakfast, was "mat class." That was where the therapists got me onto a mat and worked on my balance and stretching for an hour. At 10:00 o'clock, I had wheelchair class, where I learned how to use a manual wheelchair (although I was already adept at using my wheelchair, from going up and down the street in Dawson Springs). There were always three or four patients in each group, so I was learning with other patients who had similar injuries to mine. Lunch was great because the hospital was dealing with patients who were tremendously malnourished, so the food was delicious and nutritious. After lunch, we would repeat the first two classes and then spend thirty minutes in a "standing stall," which was designed to allow us to stand upright. Standing was good for patients' bones and had psychological benefits.

One of the reasons I especially enjoyed doing the exercises was my physical therapist, a beautiful woman named Adele Stalder. She was four years older than me and was married, so I knew she was not available, but I still wanted to impress her. Anything she asked me to do, I did it. (It's a guy thing.)

About a month before arriving in Denver, I had begun to notice improved mobility in my right arm, although it was slight. After working with Adele for a few weeks, my tricep muscles were now getting stronger. Instead of just pulling, I could raise my arm slightly, and I felt like a kid. *Wow! Look what I can do!* I was still a quadriplegic, but having partial use of even one arm suddenly made it possible to do new things.

For example, I was able to learn to transfer from the wheelchair to a bed by myself. That seemingly simple procedure required the ability to lock my elbows, scoot my butt out of the edge of the chair, put one hand on the thing that I was transferring to, and then slide the rest of the way. The first time was a little scary because I realized that if my arms gave out, I would probably crash to the floor. However, Adele was there to catch me if I fell, which gave me the confidence I needed. She would not help me transfer, but if I lost my balance, my head would go against her side. She was my safety net.

Every goal Adele put in front of me, I did my best to attain. She motivated me and pushed me to get better, the way my neighborhood friends did when we were kids, playing backyard basketball. That's what we need as humans—structure, routine, work, a sense of purpose. Every time I achieved one of Adele's challenges, I wanted to push the envelope further. I think the fact that I was an athlete helped because I was more accustomed to pushing myself. I was very competitive and always wanted to know what I could try next, which most spinal cord injury patients could not do. The answer was a floor-to-chair transfer.

To accomplish this move, I would sit on the floor with my legs crossed, lean forward, support my torso with my arms, and raise my butt from the floor to the height of the wheelchair seat. I must have looked ridiculous. It was something an Olympic gymnast could barely do. This maneuver had no practical application for me; the only reason I did it was to prove I could. I was accomplishing things that were hard. Adele even had me teach "sock class" to the other patients. For a quad, the act of putting socks on is a major challenge.

Quitting time for the physical therapists was five o'clock, but it was party time for me. The Craig Hospital had a fantastic recreation room, with pool, air hockey, and other games for patients who were able to play them. After dinner each day, I would hit the rec room and play until bedtime at eleven.

There was plenty to do on the weekends, too, like going to Denver Nuggets basketball games, the Broncos at Mile High Stadium, trips up into the mountains, watching ice hockey, even visiting the planetarium. Doing all those things created a sense of normalcy in my life. It felt good to work all day and then play at night and on weekends.

One of the big challenges for anyone, after a serious injury, is getting the courage to go out in public. Besides the obvious physical limitations, it's awkward realizing that people are always staring at you. Nowadays, it is common to see people with all kinds of disabilities out in public, but back then, it was not. When I went out with a group from Craig, the staring did not make me so uncomfortable because I was with other people.

12

ON THE ROAD AGAIN

Many people who meet me for the first time are surprised to discover that I can drive a car. They wonder how someone who cannot use his legs and has limited use of his arms can control anything except a motorized wheelchair by manipulating a toggle switch. I learned to drive at the Craig Hospital, but not before spending time at home, where the doctors sent me for six months to become acclimated to living on my own.

By the time I returned to Denver, it had been almost a year since my injury. It had also been that long since I had driven a car. Driving lessons were initially very intimidating. The training car was equipped with hand controls for braking and accelerating. Even though I could not grip the steering wheel, I was able to maneuver the car by placing my right hand on a spinner knob that was mounted on a triangular-shaped frame on the steering wheel. I used my left hand for accelerating and braking. The instructor could take over in an emergency, but otherwise, it was up to me to drive. That first day, I was so afraid. *"What happens if I get confused and do things backward?"*

At first, my biggest challenge was balance. If I turned the car too quickly, the centrifugal force would cause me to lean in the opposite direction. Left turns were especially tricky because if I leaned to the right, there was nothing to catch me. To compensate, I learned to lean in the direction of the turn, to stay upright.

The first time I drove on an interstate highway in Denver, I went about fifty miles per hour in the middle lane, with everyone else passing me at seventy miles per hour.

"I'm not going to pass you if you don't go at least sixty-five," the instructor said.

"I don't need to go that fast," I answered. "Fifty is fine."

By that point, I was fairly confident in my ability to control the vehicle. I was more concerned about what would happen if the driver in front of me slammed on his brakes. My arms were not in great shape; could I react quickly enough? The instructor explained that using my left arm and hand was probably safer than if I could use my feet because a person can move their arm more quickly and more precisely than their foot. Then, she repeated her previous warning: "You need to keep up with the traffic, or you will cause an accident. Drive faster, or you won't get your license."

Carefully, I pulled the accelerator control, my eyes darting back and forth from road to dashboard, as the speedometer crept from fifty to fifty-five, fifty-eight, sixty, sixty-three, and then, sixty-five m.p.h. It felt wonderful, gliding down the highway as fast as almost everyone else. My only fear, then, was seeing a flashing red light in the rear-view mirror. Luckily, there was no accident; not even a close call. My instructor was in the passenger's seat, but Jesus was my backseat driver.

Since first getting a driver's license at the age of sixteen, I had owned two used cars, both run-down jalopies. After getting my Driver Certification for Disabled in Denver, I returned to Kentucky and splurged on a brand-new, midnight blue Cougar RX-7 with yellow pinstripes and a moonroof. It was awesome! Medical insurance paid for the disability modifications, but I paid for the car with money I had saved up from working in the coal mine.

Learning to drive a car after becoming paralyzed was one of my greatest accomplishments since my accident. When you think about it, a vehicle makes everyone equal. People don't walk most places; they drive. A nondisabled person is just as dependent on a car getting from point A to point B safely, as much as I am. Behind the wheel, I could go anywhere. Even California.

13

PSYCHIC CONNECTION

The Bible teaches against psychics, but at the age of twenty-one, I did not know that, so when my brother-in-law, Howard, told me about a psychic healer he had heard about in Los Angeles, I was curious.

Howard had long been fascinated with Edgar Cayce, the famous clairvoyant from Kentucky, who died in 1945. That led him to read a lot of books and articles on ESP, mysticism, and such. The psychic he heard about in California was Douglas Johnson, a so-called "healer to the stars," who rose to fame after supposedly healing himself from a chronic illness when he was a child. He was involved with an organization called the Laguna Niguel "Search for God" Study Group, where he conducted healings. Some of his clients were celebrities. He seemed to have a good reputation, so I bought a couple of plane tickets and flew to LA with my mom.

I went to see Doug several times at his church. Each time, he hovered his hands about a half inch from my neck for about thirty minutes. He did not charge a set fee, but he accepted donations. I received two "treatments" a day for about a week and a half. They didn't do me any good, but they didn't hurt.

At the first service I attended, an attractive woman, who appeared to be in her early thirties, approached me and said, "Hello, little brother."

"What do you mean?" I asked.

"I noticed you, when you came in," she said. "We have lived together in past lives."

I was simultaneously freaked out and flattered. Here I was, a young guy from Podunkville, visiting Hollywood for the first time, and a beautiful woman was flirting with me. It was definitely a *"You're not in Kansas anymore"* moment!

"I'm Sylvia," she said, taking my right hand in hers. "Do you mind if I read your palm?"

Gently, she pried my fingers open and turned my hand over so my palm faced upward. After studying it for a moment, she observed that the creases in my skin formed a square with a star inside, which supposedly meant that I was Christ-like. She went on to say I had always been a "defender" in my past lives. Once, I had been an Indian warrior. Another time, I had been one of the Knights of the Round Table. I did not know much about reincarnation, but I was pretty sure it was not compatible with Christianity. I wasn't sure if she was nuts, or if I was, but I was hooked.

"You see this long line? It's your lifeline," she said. Then, pointing to a specific spot, she continued, "And here is where you became paralyzed, but I see a time in your future where you will get better."

Well, I sure liked the sound of that!

Later that week, I met another woman at the meeting who also claimed to be psychic. She asked me for a piece of jewelry to hold, so I gave her my watch. She held it tightly and closed her eyes for a moment and then proclaimed that I would be back on my feet, although she could not predict when. She also said that one day, when I was older, I would become very powerful.

All the people I met at the healing group in LA were nice, but I was skeptical of their ability to cure me. I was, however, growing more interested in Sylvia on a personal level. She claimed to be a writer and said that she wanted to write a book about me. We even went out to dinner and movies a few times. I had only planned to be in LA for ten days, but I promised her that I would return soon and stay longer.

***

After flying home, I was glad to get back into my new car. In Dawson Springs, there were places where you could park your car off to the side, facing the street. One night, I was out cruising, and I pulled over. I had the window rolled down and was relaxing, when two girls pulled up alongside me.

"Hey there, how are you doing?" the passenger asked. "I'm Carol. What's your name?"

"Ron," I said.

The cool thing about being in a car was that my wheelchair was not the first thing somebody noticed; it allowed the other person to get to know me a little bit first and not immediately judge me as a quadriplegic. Carol and her friend got out of their car and stood there, flirting with me for a few minutes, before asking why I didn't get out of mine.

"I'd love to, but believe it or not, I'm in a wheelchair," I said.

"You're joking!" Carol said.

"I wish I was."

"Where is it?" she asked.

"In the backseat," I said.

To my surprise, my condition did not seem to bother Carol. She was curious, but in a caring way. I found her to be very attractive. We exchanged phone numbers and the next thing I knew, we were dating. One night, Carol made a stunning pronouncement.

"Ronnie, I feel like the Holy Spirit told me you are going to be healed."

She was crying tears of joy, which caused me to cry tears of excitement. I am not saying she made it up or was trying to manipulate me, but her "prophesy" was exactly what I wanted to hear, and it put our relationship on a fast track. Within a few weeks, we were discussing marriage. There was just one problem—I was still dating Sylvia, the psychic, even though I had not seen her for a couple of months.

Since I had promised Sylvia I would return to LA to work on the book, I loaded up the car and headed west in my Cougar with my mom and sister, Lolo, in case I needed help. I told Carol that

I would fly her out after I got situated. I had not yet told either woman about the other.

***

When I arrived in LA, Sylvia had already found me a one-bedroom apartment in Agoura Hills, just north of Malibu. I had to pay the rent—$800 a month—but I was grateful she went to the trouble of finding me a place to live. I moved into the apartment with my mother and Lolo. Although it was cramped, it was very nice.

Living in LA was the opposite of everything I had ever known. For one thing, the mountains were brown, not lush and green like the hills in Kentucky. The air was so smoggy the first time I was there I had not noticed the mountains. And then, there was the traffic. The freeways were confusing, the way they crisscrossed and could be especially nerve-wracking during rush hour, which seemed to be all the time. It took forever to drive across town.

Sylvia and I spent a couple of months working on the book. We would get together and she would interview me on tape. There were lots of conversations and notes. There were also more dinners and movies. Since Sylvia was a psychic, I wondered if she could read my mind. If so, she did not let on if she knew about Carol! Our involvement made Carol's upcoming visit especially awkward. I did not feel like I was cheating on either girlfriend. I had never discussed a commitment with Sylvia, and even though Carol and I had discussed the possibility of marriage, it was just talk; we were not engaged.

I finally told Sylvia about Carol just before Carol flew to LA. She was not happy to hear about the competition for my affection, but she dealt with the situation maturely. I think our age difference helped.

Once in LA, it did not take long for Carol to start talking about marriage again. She moved into the apartment with my mom and me while my sister used Carol's return ticket to fly back to Dawson Springs. I don't remember who proposed to whom, but soon Carol and I were engaged.

Despite her disappointment over my relationship with Carol, Sylvia continued working with me on the book. However, $800 a month was more than I could afford for an apartment, so Mom, Carol, and I drove home. Sylvia was supposed to finish the book, but I don't think she got anywhere with it. I stayed in touch with her for a couple of years, but we drifted apart and eventually stopped talking.

Carol and I got married that October in the lodge at Pennyrile Forest State Park, just outside of Dawson Springs, in a small ceremony with about fifty guests in attendance. Mom was there along with my sisters and all seven of my nephews and nieces, but not Dad. After a two-day honeymoon nearby, the new Mrs. Adams moved into my double-wide next door to Mom.

With my head out of the clouds and my feet back in the Bluegrass, it was time to turn my attention to something more realistic than Hollywood healers and fleeting relationships with struggling screenwriters. My vocational caseworker had been pushing me to go back to school. I felt like I was not ready because I was still having problems peeing and pooping on myself and transferring in and out of my chair. Then, I remembered that "Huh" moment I had in a Louisville hospital almost two years earlier. I wasn't sure how I would take notes in class and handle the difficulties of going to school, but challenges had never stopped me before. God was on my side.

14

MAKING THE GRADE

Even though I had learned to use a motorized wheelchair in Denver, I continued using a manual chair at home for exercise. Unlike some quadriplegics, I had partial use of my triceps, the muscles used for pushing down, lifting up a chair, opening doors, and performing other basic tasks. As long as those muscles functioned, I was determined to keep them in shape.

In January of 1979, I enrolled at Madisonville Community College (MCC) because it was just twenty-five miles from home and tuition was covered by the Kentucky Office of Vocational Rehabilitation. Carol's older sister, a single mom, was also a student there. I drove her to school each day and she, in turn, helped get the wheelchair in and out of my car. To help make ends meet, Carol took a part-time accounting job.

I really wasn't sure how I would do at MCC. I had struggled academically at Cumberland College, but that was because basketball was my priority. At Madisonville, I would need to focus more on studying. I was taking eighteen credit hours per semester, plus two correspondence classes from Western Kentucky University—essentially twenty-four credit hours— eight full courses at a time. My favorite class was psychology. That first semester, I achieved a 3.9 grade point average. I was as shocked as anybody when I started getting good grades. It's amazing what you can accomplish when you get serious about something. While my classmates were out partying, I was reading the class material twice. Once, I overheard a student whisper to another, "Go ask that guy in the wheelchair; he's real smart."

My initial plan was to get an associate of business management degree, but after the first semester, I knew that a two-year degree would have limited practicality in the real world. I switched over to an associate of arts degree to earn credits that I could later transfer to a four-year university.

Meanwhile, I decided to start training for the National Wheelchair Games, which were scheduled to take place at the University of Illinois Urbana-Champaign in March of 1980. I was already in pretty good shape from rolling up and down the hill on my street, but I started working out more consistently and got to be pretty fast. Still, I had never been much of a track person, and I was competing against more experienced athletes, so I was surprised when I made it to the finals of the hundred-meter dash. I would be racing against seven other finalists.

After sitting around for a couple of hours, waiting for the event, my adrenaline had built up and I was raring to go. When the starting gun fired, I pushed so hard that my chair popped

Ron competing in the 24th National Wheelchair Games at the University of Illinois Urbana-Champaign, 1980.

a wheelie and almost flipped over backward. I eased off just enough to let the chair fall back on all fours, but those three or four seconds cost me valuable time and I was already ten yards behind the second-to-last-place racer by the time I got going. I pushed as hard as I could and finished in sixth place, which wasn't too bad, considering my clumsy start.

Meanwhile, cracks were starting to develop in my marriage. After Carol and I had been married for about six months, we drove to Denver for my annual evaluation at the Craig Hospital. We checked into a nearby apartment, which the hospital owned for use by visiting patients and their families. One night, we got into an argument while walking a couple of blocks from the hospital. I don't remember what it was about, but things became so heated that Carol stormed off and left me on the sidewalk. Back then, there were no curb breaks for wheelchairs, so I asked a stranger to help get my chair onto the street. The chair was not motorized, so I manually wheeled myself back to the apartment several blocks away.

The street was not busy with traffic. What occurred at that moment was more of an inconvenience than a safety issue. I know the Bible teaches that marriage is supposed to be forever, but when Carol abandoned me on that sidewalk a thousand miles from home, it caused me to think, for the first time, that maybe our marriage was not a good idea. I became certain of our incompatibility a few months later.

Quads are prone to kidney and bladder infections, so my doctor had ordered me to drink cranberry juice—a natural diuretic—several times a day. One day Carol and I were relaxing at home in our double-wide, next door to Mom's house. I don't remember why, but Carol was in a bad mood and would not bring me a glass of juice. I could not reach it myself, so I called Mom.

"Would you mind coming over and getting me some cranberry juice?" I asked.

"Isn't Carol there?"

"Yeah, but she's upset about something and she won't get it for me," I said.

A minute later, Mom showed up at the backdoor, but Carol blocked her from coming in.

"You stay out of this!" Carol said.

"Move out of my way!" Mom demanded.

I had never seen her so angry. She forced her way in, like a football player pushing through an offensive line. Carol, who was holding a glass of water, splashed it in Mom's face, and that's when the fur started flying—literally! I'm not sure who went first, but Mom and Carol suddenly were pulling each other's hair and yelling, crashing into furniture and falling to the floor, rolling around like a couple of WWA wrestlers. I was terrified someone would get hurt and was frustrated I could not intervene as I had a couple of years before, when Dad attacked Mom. After about ten minutes, the fight ended, more out of exhaustion than with either woman winning. I went home with Mom, leaving Carol in the trailer, and filed for divorce five days later.

Could the marriage have been saved with counseling? I have no idea, but at that time, neither of us was in a mood to find out. I chalked up our problems to mutual immaturity and perhaps my misguided belief that just because Carol once told me that God had spoken to her about me, it was a sign that we were meant for each other. We clearly were not.

15

ANIMAL HOUSE

By the time I graduated from Madisonville Community College in May of 1980, I was physically and mentally exhausted. In just seventeen months, I had earned sixty-one credit hours, with a 3.8 grade point average.

I enrolled as a junior at Murray State University, seventy-three miles southwest of Dawson Springs, majoring in Business Administration with an emphasis on management. My decision to go there came after much discussion, at different times, with various people, most notably David Massamore, my family's attorney. He was an alumnus of MSU, where he had belonged to the Sigma Nu fraternity. When he learned I had decided on MSU, he offered to pay my national dues for Sigma Nu if I would join the fraternity and help get it back on its feet. I agreed, but did not fully grasp the enormity of the fraternity's dysfunction until I arrived.

Remember the movie *Animal House*? That pretty well represents what was going on at the Sigma Nu frat house at Murray State in 1980. Drinking and carousing were all anyone wanted to do. Since I did not drink, I stuck out like a glass of milk in a saloon. I was easily elected president of the Murray State chapter because nobody cared to run against me, but the members had no interest in my suggestions for improving their image. I was a captain without a crew, like Captain Bligh in *Mutiny on the Bounty*. After less than a year, I resigned from

Sigma Nu. The last I heard, the Murray State chapter had shut down.

Except for Sigma Nu, I have mostly good memories of Murray State. During my first semester, I decided to take it easy and signed up for just fifteen credit hours. I went Monday, Wednesday, and Friday, driving each of those days from Dawson Springs. My niece, Beth, was also attending Murray State, so she rode with me. Even though she spent most of her free time with her boyfriend, she was available to help if I needed her.

I made pretty much all B's during my first semester and was getting comfortable with the routine of going to classes, so I started taking a full load in the second semester. The commute was getting to be a hassle, so I moved to a trailer park in Murray. Over the next two years, the professors and other students treated me well, and I made a lot of friends, including one I will call Emily.

Emily was in a couple of my business classes and was very attractive. She was also very engaged, but that did not stop her from coming over to my trailer to study. One thing led to another, and before long, we became romantically involved. She said she was going to break off her engagement with the other guy. I told her that would have to be her decision.

One night, she called me on the phone.

"Ronnie, it's Emily. We need to talk," she said. (You know it's bad news when someone says that.)

"What about?" I asked.

"I'm going to have to stop seeing you. I'm so sorry."

"What happened? I thought things were okay between us," I said.

"It has nothing to do with you, Ronnie," she said. "The other guy I've been seeing is weak. He needs me."

"But I need you."

"If I leave him, he'll be crushed," Emily said. "You're strong, Ronnie. You'll be fine. I know you will. I have confidence in you."

How could I be strong, but still lose? I had previously broken up with a high school sweetheart and divorced my first wife, but being cut loose by Emily over the phone, threw me into the worst depression I had ever been in. Being in a college environment where everyone else was young and active highlighted my physical limitations in a way I had not felt before. I was pretty sure my wheelchair had more to do with Emily leaving me than any sense of responsibility she felt for her other boyfriend. I guess I should have known better than to paint myself into a corner of a lovers' triangle.

My mom became so worried about me that, unbeknownst to me, she got some kind of antidepressant drug and conspired with my niece to sneak it into my other pills. I felt better for a while, but then I felt even worse than before after discovering that I had been drugged against my will. I went to see a counselor at the college.

"Where do you feel the most safe and secure?" he asked.

I thought for a moment and answered, "I'm always that way when I'm around my mom" (even though she was the one who came up with the idea to drug me).

"Well then, every Friday, instead of just sitting around here all weekend, why don't you go home and do things?"

That was good advice, I thought. For the next couple of months, I slid behind the wheel of my Cougar XR7 every Friday, after my last class, and drove to Dawson Springs, where Mom always had my favorite dinner prepared. Dad was living with Mom again and was behaving himself, but still was not real friendly. He would usually eat dinner with us and then retreat to the bedroom, where he listened to country music or talk radio while Mom and I watched movies on TV late into the night.

16

THE 10K

Just as I had figured out that crying would not do any good, I decided that being depressed was pointless. I threw myself back into studying to get my mind back on more productive things at Murray State.

One night I was reading in the university library when another student came over to my table and sat across from me. Her name was Amy. She appeared tomboyish, but she was attractive. Unlike most of the other female students, she did not wear makeup, and she wore clothes most people would probably consider frumpy. She was totally uninhibited and did not care what other people thought about her appearance, which I thought was refreshing. She also did not mind that I was in a wheelchair.

"How would you like me to come to your house and fix you dinner?" she asked.

Amy was majoring in nutrition or something like that, so I figured she must be a good cook, and she was friendly and pretty, so of course, I accepted her offer. I was surprised when she arrived at my trailer the next night, riding a bicycle and carrying all the ingredients for our meal in a backpack. She cooked a delicious spaghetti dinner and we talked for hours. She was a free spirit, sort of a hippy, completely unlike any of my previous girlfriends.

Not only was Amy an avid bicyclist, but she was also a runner. When she told me she and one of her girlfriends were going to run a 10K race in Louisville, I wanted to do it, too. A 10K is a little over six miles, which is a long way to push a wheelchair when you've only done a hundred-yard dash, but after my mediocre performance in the National Wheelchair Games, I needed to prove myself. I had no idea what I was about to get into.

March 14, 1981, was the date of the first annual Rodes City Run 10K, which has since become a major race in the region. The starting line was in front of the Galt House, a luxury hotel in downtown Louisville. There were about 2,000 participants. I was the only one in a wheelchair. It was a cool day, so I was not worried about becoming overheated. However, the beginning of the race was downhill toward the Ohio River. The slope was only a block long, but I had never tried to control my chair on such a steep hill and did not realize how risky it was. Looking back on it, I am surprised the race officials let me do it, especially since I had not registered.

Almost immediately, I started rolling downhill faster than I had ever gone in my chair. I was ahead of some of the runners at first, but my life flashed before my eyes. There was a sharp turn at the bottom of the hill, so I knew I needed to slow down, or I would surely flip over. Despite wearing a double set of gloves, as I pressed on the wheels, the friction was so strong that it almost tore one of the gloves off. I was able to slow down just in time to avoid an accident, but by the time I reached the first turn, all the runners had left me in the dust. I kept going.

About a quarter of a mile up the road, the police escort at the rear needed to make a decision about whether to stay with me or catch up with the runners, who were far ahead by now. The escort sped up to catch up with the runners, leaving me alone in the middle of a two-lane road. Motorists were now starting to drive on the road in both directions while I pushed my wheelchair along the double-yellow line between them. A motorcycle cop circled around and came back alongside me.

"Hey, buddy!" he shouted, over the roar of his engine, "One of the runners just crossed the finish line, so you can go ahead and quit now!"

"I don't…think you…understand!" I shouted with each push. "I didn't…come…to win! I came…to finish!"

The cop just shook his head as he waved me on and drove away. My arms and shoulders burned from the strain. I was thirstier than I had ever been, but unlike runners, I could not grab a drink and slug it down, because if I got my gloves wet they would be too slippery for me to push the wheels.

"The guy in the wheelchair's still going," squawked a tinny voice over a walkie-talkie, somewhere off to the side. *"Keep the road closed."*

After about twenty-five minutes, I reached the halfway point and started noticing runners who had stopped, some of them bent over, throwing up on the pavement. I had never been so happy to see sick people. *They* had given up, but *I* was still in the race! I wish I could tell you that I prayed for them, but my only thought at that moment was to keep going. I was not going to win, but at least I would not come in last place!

Two miles later, I came to a hill I would have to climb before the final stretch. It was so steep that every time I pushed hard, the chair almost flipped over backward, so I pushed short, climbing just a few inches at a time. Each push was like two steps forward and one step back, but I was making progress. My shoulders felt as if sharp knives were stabbing them. Despite being exhausted, I could not stop now.

As I crested the hill, I saw the Galt House a half-mile ahead. The street was still shut down, just for me. Twenty thousand spectators were cheering and clapping as I pushed along the yellow line. A blister the size of a half-dollar had formed on my right hand, but I ignored the pain. Crossing the finish line, I felt higher than the time when I made that game-winning shot on the basketball court in the sixth grade. I might not have won the race in Louisville that day, but by the grace of God, I finished.

After resting for a while, Amy, her girlfriend, and I went to a shopping mall. I had brought both my racing chair and my regular chair to Louisville, so Amy got in one and rode around behind me at the mall as if we were a train. We looked like a couple of kids. People stared, but Amy didn't care and neither did I. We were having fun. "The guy in the wheelchair" was in love.

17

LEGAL EAGLE

Amy and I dated for the next few months, and everything was going great until her family found out about me. She had a lot of brothers and sisters, and they were dead set against her being tied to someone with physical limitations. In other words, *she could do better*. She was angry at their unaccepting attitude, but it became such an issue I decided to end the relationship. She might have stayed with me despite her family's objections, but I did not want to be responsible for the rift it would have caused. As with previous breakups, I felt like damaged goods. The lyrics to Dan Fogelberg's classic song "Another Auld Lang Syne" ran through my head: *"Just for a moment I was back at school / And felt that old familiar pain / And, as I turned to make my way back home / The snow turned into rain."*

I dealt with the sadness of losing Amy the way I had always coped with depression—instead of moping around and feeling sorry for myself, I decided to stay busy, to keep my mind occupied. That wasn't hard to do with classes and homework. Oh, yeah, I also bought a Corvette—a silver-blue, 1981 model with V-8 engine, automatic transmission, power steering, power 4-wheel disc brakes, air conditioning, power windows and locks, CD player, T-tops and 15" aluminum wheels. You might wonder how a poor college student could afford such a car. Well, back then, a new Corvette cost about $16,000. I was receiving monthly disability checks of about $700, plus I had saved a good amount of money while working in the coal mine. Also, I was debt-free, so I was able to get a loan easily.

Even though I was able to afford the Corvette, it was the most impractical thing I had ever bought in my life and made absolutely no sense. It was hard to get into the driver's seat and there was not enough room for my chair, but I sure looked cool, driving around! I even got another girlfriend, but she soon moved to Nashville, so I knew that relationship was not going to work out. I think she only liked me for my 'Vette.

During the last few months of my senior year, I became a salesman for Amway, the company known for beauty, health, and homecare products. My dentist, who was an Amway representative, convinced me I could make a lot of money by selling the company's products by signing people up as distributors. The goal was to get six friends or family members to buy one hundred dollars' worth of products. That was your "downline." Each of them, in turn, would get six people in *their* downline to buy one-hundred dollars' worth of products, and so on. It seemed simple. Everybody knows at least six people, right? It was classic multilevel marketing, which meant the higher up in the organization you were, the more money you could make. At least, until the pool of available recruits ran out.

During what little spare time I had between classes and homework, I would drive as far as seventy miles one way, selling Amway products to my distributors and attending motivational seminars, most of which were small gatherings. One such meeting was in a second-floor apartment, which could only be reached by going up a steep flight of wooden steps outside the building. Three men heaved me up those narrow steps, stopping along the way to rest, barely keeping from dropping me as my wheelchair hung precariously over the edge. At another meeting, a top Amway distributor showed up driving a Ferrari and wearing an expensive-looking pin-stripe suit. He was a millionaire and showed pictures of his beautiful house and talked about how anyone could become as rich as he was if they had two-hundred-sixteen people in their downline. Like the time I tried going into the rabbit-breeding business as a boy, dollar signs flashed in front of my eyes.

Within two months, I rose to what Amway called "pin level," which meant that I had successfully recruited a lot of people who also had recruited people. I was invited to an Amway convention in Orlando (at my own expense), where I gave a pep talk in front of 10,000 people. It was my first time doing any kind of public speaking, except for a speech class in college. I loved it. The idea of so many people being interested in what I had to say was a boost to my ego.

However, despite my hard work, I was spending more money driving around Western Kentucky to meet with recruits and attend seminars than I was making in commissions. After three or four months, people in my downline were becoming discouraged and leaving the program. I was never able to gain the kind of traction I would need to make the system work for me, so I quit.

I know that Amway is controversial. Many people consider it a pyramid scheme. I am not saying it is. Amway makes good products, and many people earn a good living with the company, but it takes real commitment and a willingness to stick with it for a long time. It also helps if you have lots of friends who have families who can use one hundred dollars' worth of household products per month, which I did not. The company simply was not a good fit for me at that time in my life.

After graduating from Murray State in August of 1982, the reality hit me that job opportunities for a quadriplegic might be somewhat limited. I had a college degree, which in and of itself was pretty remarkable, but even though I had graduated with a respectable 3.6 grade point average, I still did not have any "wow" skills that would get me noticed by employers.

As I pondered my next move, I thought back to that "Huh" moment at The Rehabilitation Center in Louisville, where a psychiatrist suggested I might be able to go to law school. I had already lived pretty much on my own for almost a year and a half at Murray State, so that was the least of my worries. I was more concerned about the rigorous academic demands of law school. For starters, I would first have to take a Law School Admission Test (LSAT), which is incredibly complicated. I was not prepared to jump back into an academic environment immediately, so I signed up to take the LSAT in December and began studying for it in October.

Meanwhile, I decided to put my new bachelor's degree and Amway experience to good use by starting a T-shirt and sports uniform business in Madisonville because it was a bigger town than Dawson Springs and was nearby. I bought a little storefront building that had a house in the back to live in and invested about $2,000 in the initial inventory. The profit margin was small, but I made up for it in volume. That first year, I provided uniforms for about thirty softball teams and silkscreened about a thousand T-shirts. A couple of family members worked for me, including my brother-in-law, Richard. He worked at the coal mine, but he needed a temporary job because the United Mine Workers were on strike.

I also invested in a small house in Dawson Springs, which had some fire damage, but not too bad. I paid $28,000, planning to fix it and flip it. Richard was good at construction, so he agreed to handle the renovation work in exchange for splitting the profit. When the work was finished, he and Lolo put a "for sale" sign in the yard. A week later, I called Mom, just to say hi.

"Ronnie, your Dad wants to talk to you," she said, as she handed the phone over to him.

"Hey, Ron, I just thought you might want to know I bought that house that Richard's been working on."

"You mean over on Frederick Road?" I asked.

"Yep, just bought it today. Gonna move in next week."

Dad had no clue he had just bought a house from his own son. My name was on the Contract of Sale, but Dad's eyesight was poor, so he probably did not see it. Mom knew I was the seller, but she did not tell Dad, and neither did Richard or Lolo because of Dad's erratic, irrational behavior. The less anyone told him about my personal business, the better. He was in a good mood at that moment, but I knew from experience it could change in an instant.

"That's a real nice house, Dad," I said. "Congratulations."

Dad came and went through the years, but he and Mom lived in that house for the rest of their lives. Richard had done a great job fixing it up.

When December arrived, it came time for me to take the LSAT. As expected, the exam was hard, but you know what helped? All those chess games that I played with my cousin, Billy Deane, during the first couple of years after I was released from rehab in Louisville! One part of the LSAT was the Analytical Reasoning section, which is more commonly called "logic games." In each logic game, a scenario is described, and the test-taker is required to answer five to eight questions by following a unique set of rules. The purpose is to measure the student's analytical skills under varying circumstances.

Before my accident, I could think quickly on the basketball court in the heat of a game, but outside the gymnasium, I was not very good at long-range, contemplative analysis. Chess changed that. It is a great thinking game, and when I started playing it with Billy, my brain got so much more exercise than ever before, as I was forced to think several moves ahead. Chess is applicable to so many aspects of life.

I hardly aced the LSAT, but I did not do as badly as I expected. My score was somewhere in the middle, which meant I probably would not qualify for Harvard or Yale, but I might get into a lesser-known school. I gathered up all my letters of reference, college transcripts, and LSAT results and sent them to the Salmon P. Chase College of Law at Northern Kentucky University (now known as NKU Chase College of Law). The school had an excellent reputation, it was not that far from home (just 250 miles to the northeast), and it was affordable.

I was both euphoric and intimidated when I received my acceptance letter on June 1, 1983. It was cool to think I would finally get onto that playing field, but I also had plenty of personal doubts. An annoying little voice kept whispering things like, *"You only got accepted because they needed a token wheelchair boy."*

Satan plays tricks that way with his lies and personal insults that cause you to belittle yourself. He had been telling me I wasn't good enough my whole life, but despite all the challenges, I had always pushed through with God's help. Now I was determined to make it through law school.

Ron Adams (front) with Richard Hinton (brother-in-law), Ruth Adams (mother), Joyce Boucher (sister) and Delores Hinton (sister).

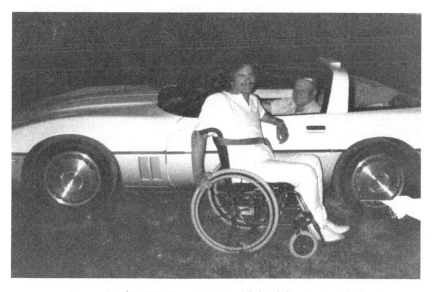

Ron next to his 1981 Corvette. Seated behind the steering wheel: Ron's father, Walter Adams.

18

THE CHASE AND JOURNEY

Chase College of Law was founded in Cincinnati, Ohio in 1893, but relocated across the Ohio River to Northern Kentucky in 1972. The school was named after U.S. Chief Justice Salmon P. Chase, a well-known abolitionist who was appointed to the Supreme Court by Abraham Lincoln. Before entering politics, he was known for defending escaped slaves.

I moved into a dorm on campus and started law school in August of 1983. There were about twenty-five other law students in my dorm, all roughly my age and seemingly with big egos. Or, maybe that was just my initial knee-jerk impression because they were good-looking and not in wheelchairs. I was already feeling like I must be the dumbest person in the building, especially after discovering many of my classmates had parents who were lawyers.

My first week at Chase was Introduction to Law Week. At the end of Introduction to Law class on Thursday, I told the professor I could not write very easily because my fingers could not grip a pen and I asked if I could dictate an exam that was scheduled for the next night.

"You won't need to dictate," he said. "The exam is easy. It shouldn't take more than thirty minutes."

The breath was knocked out of me the next evening when the prof handed me thirty pages. *"I can't even read thirty pages in thirty minutes,"* I thought. I knew right then and there that I was in deep doo-doo. Luckily, it was a three-hour, not thirty-minute test. I struggled through every second and was still working on answers when the professor called time at 9:30. I was not quite finished.

I knew I had not done well. All the self-doubt I had ever felt in my life came flooding back as I left the classroom. Pushing back to the dorm alone, I was so depressed and consumed by fear of failure that I was not paying attention and almost got hit by a car while crossing a street.

You know that song, "You're No Good?" I heard a voice singing it, only it wasn't Linda Ronstadt; it was Satan. I had heard those words my whole life and I sang along, over and over: *You're no good, you're no good, baby you're no good.* Just like a catchy melody, a negative message becomes embedded in your mind when you play it often enough. At that moment, the Devil was perched on my shoulder, serenading me again.

"Shut up!" I said. "I'm not listening to you!"

Now I was angry. How many times had people or circumstances held me down, making me think I wasn't good enough; making me feel that I didn't deserve good things? Hadn't I pushed through and succeeded, anyway? In high school, I never would have considered quitting basketball just because I missed a shot or my team lost a game. I might have screwed up on my first law school exam, but there would be others. I would just have to study harder. *"I am in law school,"* I thought. *"I made it this far and I'm not quitting!"*

***

Now that I was living in Northern Kentucky, I put my brother-in-law, Richard, in charge of the T-shirt business back in Madisonville. One night, while I was studying in my dorm, the phone rang.

"Hey, Ronnie, it's Richard."

"Yeah, what's going on?" I asked.

"Something kind of interesting happened today," he said. "A big tour bus stopped outside the shop and some guys with a band came in and bought a bunch of shirts."

"What band?"

"I forget," Richard said. "It had something to do with being out on the road, like 'Travel' or 'Adventure.' I'm not sure, maybe 'Journey.' That's it! Did you ever hear of a band called Journey?"

"JOURNEY?" I blurted, dumbfounded. "Are you telling me that JOURNEY, the *band*, actually stopped at our shop and bought T-shirts?"

"Yeah, about four hundred dollars' worth," Richard said.

I pinched myself to make sure that I wasn't dreaming.

"Well, what then? Did you get them to sign a shirt or a picture or something?"

"No," Richard said. "Should I?"

"Oh, man!" I was bummed out.

Here it was, 1983. By then, Journey had already had two of the biggest hit singles in recent rock music history—"Don't Stop Believin'" and "Open Arms," from their 1981 *Billboard* number-one album *Escape*—and my brother-in-law did not know who they were! How one of the world's most famous rock bands happened to be driving through Madisonville, Kentucky, I never found out (although they were on a national tour at that time, promoting their new album, *Frontiers*). But one of the highlights of my life—and greatest disappointments—was knowing that one of my favorite bands had come into my little store while I was 250 miles away at law school.

Steve Perry[8], if you are reading this, I hope you know that I have never stopped believing and I am still holding onto that feeling.

---

8   Former lead singer with Journey.

19

LAW SCHOOL

Question: What's the difference between a good lawyer and a bad one?
Answer: A bad lawyer can let a case drag out for several years. A good one can make it last even longer.

Law school was all-business from the get-go; no warm and fuzzy welcome reception where everybody got acquainted over punch and cookies (although beer seemed to be a much-enjoyed beverage by many students on weekends). Future lawyers were expected to hit the ground running.

The first week, I was assigned sixty pages to read and fourteen cases to brief. I had three classes, all at night. On Monday, I had Contract Law from 6:30 until 9:15. On Wednesday, Tort Law. On Friday, Property Law. Three classes might sound easy, but I needed every spare minute outside of class for studying and dealing with personal and logistical issues related to my paralysis.

My Tort professor was brilliant, but also could be intimidating. David Elder stood about six feet four inches tall and probably weighed two hundred-sixty pounds or so. He had red hair and a full beard to match and a vocabulary that would put Clarence Darrow to shame. He had his own private booth in the law library on campus, where he studied about five or six hours every day.

Professor Elder passed out a paper explaining the grading system. It said that Chase College of Law wanted to become known as "the Harvard on the Ohio." Because of that, the new class was required to have a mean grade-point average of 2.2. That meant that if the average grade was 2.2, any student with less than a 2.0 would be placed on probation and would be at greater risk of being dismissed. I might not have known anything about the law, but I knew something about math, so it wasn't hard to figure that if the average GPA is 2.2, that means a lot of students are below 2. To make things even more stressful, the paper explained that Professor Elder used the Socratic Method, which meant he could call on any student at any time, and if he deemed that student to be unprepared, the student's final grade point could be dropped by 0.5, the equivalent of half a letter grade. In other words, even if I was an average student, if I could not answer a single question to the professor's satisfaction, I could end up with a 1.7 GPA and would be out the door. It seemed arbitrary, but that's how it was.

I had never heard of the Socratic Method, but it is common at many law schools. It is a back-and-forth discussion between the teacher and student for the purpose of challenging the student's point of view and understanding of the law. As much as I enjoyed David Elder's lectures, I thought if I avoided making direct eye contact, he might not call on me. During the second week of class, my "no eye contact" strategy failed.

"Mr. Adams," Professor Elder said, "in Manhattan v. Bronx, did the appellate court bridge the possibility that the lower court ruling was arbitrary and capricious?"

"Say what?" I thought as my heart pounded and all eyes in the classroom were on me.

Back in Dawson Springs, nobody talked like that, and even during my nearly two years at Murray State University, I had never heard the word "capricious." Somehow, I ad-libbed a response that must have made sense because Professor Elder moved on to the next student. However, I realized I had better learn the nomenclature of law very quickly, or I would fail.

From then on, whenever I heard a word that I did not understand, I made an audio note of it in my tape recorder and looked it up later. I also read all class material twice, as I had done at Murray State, except this time, it was harder and took longer, and the threat of being kicked out of law school lurked around every corner of every classroom. After all that work, I would go into class thinking I understood the material, only to leave at the end of class, realizing how little I knew. My next-door neighbor in the dorm, who was a second-year student, gave me good advice.

"You need to pace yourself," he said. "Law school is a marathon, not a sprint. You've got to save yourself for the end-of-semester exam."

It sounded like good advice. I thought back to the 10K in Louisville; how I had finished the race by pushing a little bit each time and not quitting, even when it seemed nearly impossible to keep going. I would apply the same principle to law school and the upcoming end-of-semester exam.

Unlike with other types of college classes, you don't take a lot of little tests in law school; there's just one big exam in each class, at the end of the semester, which covers everything. I had fifteen or sixteen weeks of class, three classes each week, with each class about three hours long; basically, nine hours of class per week. That doesn't sound like much, but I studied eighteen to twenty-five hours each week, just to prepare. That was a lot of mental stretching for someone who never studied very hard in high school.

Final exams for the first semester were still three months away, but I knew I would have a hard time, not just with the material, but logistically. I learned the exams were structured sort of like the TV show *Jeopardy*—they would give you the answer, and then you had to figure out the question, but the question had to be written in the form of an essay. Each exam would consist of more than seven hundred pages of text. Since I was unable to hold a pen very well, I asked Professor Elder if I could dictate my answers into a tape recorder. To my great disappointment, he said no, but he offered a compromise.

"Your answers need to be in writing, but I'll tell you what," he said. "If the other professors are okay with it, you can dictate to an undergrad, who needs work-study hours."

I got together with that student to figure out the process. Since she did not know shorthand, she wrote everything in longhand, which meant I had to speak slowly to make sure she got all the words. I was not comfortable with the arrangement. Not only would it take me longer to finish each exam, but I would not have an opportunity to proof the notes. If my amanuensis[9] misunderstood me and wrote something incorrectly, I would be graded not according to my mistakes, but hers. As it turned out, she did not make any significant mistakes, but the overall process slowed me down considerably and impeded the quality of my answers.

Around the end of October, I received a note summoning me to the Dean's office regarding the results of the Introduction to Law exam, which I had taken at the end of the first week. The maximum possible score was two hundred. A minimum passing score was fifty. I got seventeen. At the top of the first page, the professor had written in red ink, *"Incredibly poor. Student should consider other career objectives."*

My heart sank. I returned to my dorm room, feeling numb, dumb, and worthless, as I had so many times before. Life sucked all over again. What could I do now? There was that voice— *"You're no good,"* except this time, it wasn't just my imagination—it was in writing. A professor had not just given me a bad grade; he had said I was not good enough to be a lawyer. Then it occurred to me—I had not yet failed at law school. I had only failed one test. There would be others.

I thought back to the day when a doctor told me I would never be any better, that I would never walk again. I had cried for hours, but then realized that crying was not doing me any good. Dropping out of law school would not do me any good, either. Moving forward did not appear promising, but at least I still had a shot, like that time in the sixth grade when the coach tipped the basketball to me, with four seconds left on the clock, and I scored the winning points. Taking myself off the playing field meant that I would definitely lose. I was not about to go down without a fight.

---

9   Someone who takes dictation.

From then on, I studied ten hours every day, and when December came, I took the final exam. For five hours, I sat in a separate room, dictating essay answers to my new undergraduate "assistant," who dutifully wrote down every word. Then, I wished her a Merry Christmas, pushed myself to my car, and drove home for the holidays.

20

NEW YEAR, NEW START

I did not feel as pessimistic about the end-of-semester exam as I had felt about the first test during my first week of law school, but I wasn't exactly feeling confident. I spent Christmas break second-guessing my answers, obsessing over whether I should have phrased certain sentences differently or cited different laws or court rulings, or whatever. I could not get the exam out of my mind.

After New Year's Day, the first week back at school felt like a deathwatch. The final exam grades were to come out the following week, which meant some students would be terminated. It was just a question of which of us would be sentenced to hang.

Chase used a letter grading system, with each letter worth a certain number of points. An "A" was worth 4, "B" was worth 3, "C" was 2, and "D" was 1. You could also get a "plus," which was worth a half-point. So, for example, an A+ would be worth 4.5 points, a B+ was worth 3.5 points, and so on.

Well, I got a C in Contracts, which was worth 2.0 points—not great, but not too bad. I got a C+ in Property, which was worth 2.5. Then, the wind got knocked out of me when my Torts exam came back with a D+, worth just 1.5. Averaged together, I had a 2. Below a 2 would have meant probation. I felt bummed out because I was on the bottom rung, but at least I was not on probation. Everyone who got below 1.5 was told to pack their belongings.

I ranked 56 out of 106, meaning there were fifty people below me, most of whom failed. It was sad to see many of my friends leaving school involuntarily. I felt guilty, knowing some students who had done better than I did on that first-week exam were now getting kicked out of law school because they failed the final exam. I had almost failed. *How could I possibly study harder?* I could only imagine what the winter semester would be like.

My classes were the same as before, with the same professors and just as much pressure, but I was starting to figure out a study routine that worked for me. In Torts class, Professor Elder called on me a lot. Surprisingly, my verbal answers usually satisfied him. Unfortunately, when it came time for the second-semester final exam, he was unimpressed with my written responses, and he gave me another D+. Fortunately, I got another C in Contracts and a C+ in Property Law, so I was still hanging on, even if by a thread. By now, I was so used to being kicked for so long I was starting to derive a certain degree of masochistic pleasure from it. Just surviving the torture seemed like a victory.

Besides the academic rigors and the logistical difficulties of maneuvering around campus, there were hardships in my dorm. It took time, but I was able to get myself dressed and do the usual personal hygiene things other people do, as well as things most other people don't have to do, like strapping on, emptying, and cleaning catheter bags.

One day, while getting ready to take a shower, I started to transfer from my bed to the shower chair when I fell to the floor. The shower chair was similar to a regular wheelchair, but it was made with stainless steel components and had a hole in the seat for when nature called. Naked and unable to reach the phone to call for help, I realized there was just one thing to do. With all the strength I could muster, I raised my arms as best I could and pushed the mattress a few inches at a time until it was three feet away from the edge of the box springs. Then, using a modified version of the floor-to-chair technique that I had learned almost seven years earlier at the Craig Hospital in Denver, I managed to maneuver up onto the box springs. By now, the mattress was in such a position that I could not have easily gotten into the shower chair. I inched up onto the mattress and scooted to the other side of the bed, where my regular wheelchair was parked. However, when I went to slide into the wheelchair, I failed to take into account the fact that the mattress was overhanging the box springs on that side of the bed. As I leaned forward and scooted my butt into position on the mattress, I fell forward and hit my head on the wheelchair's foot rests, which were in the "up" position, leaving a gash on my forehead.

After regaining my composure, I finally got into the wheelchair, draped a towel over my lap, and wheeled myself across the hall to the communal shower. The ordeal lasted about an hour. I could have yelled for help and somebody would have eventually gotten the dorm manager to open my door and rescue me, but my foolish pride told me to keep my mouth shut, even with a bloody forehead. I cleaned myself up, got dressed, and studied the rest of the day until my evening class.

One thing that I could not do was open screw-off caps on beverage containers, so twice a day, I would go through fast-food drive-throughs and order soft drinks because it was easier to sip soft drinks through a straw. It's amazing I did not get sick or gain weight that first year, considering all the McDonald's, Hardee's, and Wendy's that I ate, and the fact that I usually did not wear a coat outside during the winter, even in bitter cold. I found the coat too cumbersome to put on or take off while transferring in and out of my car. I suppose all the pushing from my dorm to the car, and then from the car to one classroom and the next, burned off the excess calories and helped keep me in shape.

Most law students were required to take summer classes, so in the summer of 1984, I took two classes, one of which met on Monday and Wednesday nights, while the other one met every Tuesday and Thursday night. Even though I had just two classes, they involved more total hours and had a heavier workload because we had to get through them in seven or eight weeks instead of the usual sixteen.

Despite the intense workload, I had some spare time that summer. I was casually dating a couple of women I met at school (yes, they knew about each other) and I was looking the best I ever had since my accident, but the wheelchair was still holding me back in almost every way. I heard about a self-help program called Silva Mind Control, which was taught across the river in Cincinnati, and purported to teach visualization techniques to improve mental function and solve problems.

Silva Mind Control was developed in the 1940s by José Silva, an electrician interested in religion, psychology, and parapsychology. He was not a doctor, but he did research on the brain to test his methods, which he claimed could help people enter states of awareness, enabling them to mentally project their thoughts and turn them into reality. His beliefs about the brain have largely been discredited. Silva Mind Control has since been rebranded as The Silva Method™, probably because "mind control" has such a creepy connotation. However, in 1984, I was just starting to learn about it.

"What if there's really something to Silva Mind Control?" I thought. *"If I could just use my brain to heal myself, everything would be great."*

I decided to check it out.

21

Second Year Law

Having survived the first year of law school, albeit by the skin of my teeth, I was feeling confident by the end of summer 1984. Going into the Fall semester, I would have new classes with different professors than before. As a second-year student, I would also be permitted to get out of the cramped dorm and live off-campus.

I found a ground-floor apartment in Cold Spring, Kentucky, a small municipality near NKU, and negotiated a deal with the landlord: If he would take the bathtub out and replace it with a wheelchair-accessible shower, I would sign an eighteen-month lease. After he agreed to my request, we each signed on the dotted line and I moved in.

The apartment was a one-bedroom efficiency. It was roomier than my dorm, but still compact enough to make it easy for me to get around. The kitchen and living room were together, so I arranged everything for easy access.

After moving in, I discovered my neighbor across the hall was my former next-door neighbor in the dorm. John Parsons was a year ahead of me at law school and a little older. He was so quiet we hardly talked when we lived on campus. Maybe because there were fewer distractions in the apartment building, we found time to get to know each other better. He would come over and we would talk about law and life. He was ultra-conservative and a little bit quirky, but super nice. In the winter, whenever it snowed, I would wake up to find that John had already shoveled a path to my car.

John was one of the few people I would invite into my apartment. I liked having friends, but I rarely invited them over because someone would inadvertently touch something or move it to where I could not reach it.

Living alone was becoming easier. I could now get dressed and into my chair in about ten minutes, which was a substantial improvement over the forty-five minutes it used to take me just to put my pants on. I also finally mastered the art of doing my bowel programs. Basically, the procedure involved defecating into a specially designed plastic bag, folding it over and sliding it out of the way before getting into the shower. I would empty and clean the bag later.

I had been reading the Bible more and more, still hoping for a miracle. One verse I kept returning to was Mark 11:23— *"Whosoever shall say unto this mountain, Be thou removed, and be thou cast into the sea; and shall not doubt in his heart, but shall believe that those things which he saith shall come to pass; he shall have whatsoever he saith."* I felt if I believed sincerely enough and could see it in my mind, I might be healed. That was one reason I signed up for the Silva Mind Control class, although I later came to realize their teachings were not compatible with Christianity.

One of the things I had been doing for several months was to record affirmations on my tape recorder. These were positive thoughts which when repeated over and over were intended to strengthen my faith and self-confidence. I also practiced a "mirror technique" taught by Silva Mind Control, which involved gazing at myself in a mirror and verbalizing what I believed. The technique was a bit like the "Stuart Smalley" affirmations, as performed by Al Franken on *Saturday Night Live* in the 1990s. Hopefully, mine were not so absurd, although I imagine if you had seen me doing them, you might think otherwise.

My classes during the fall semester that year were Civil Procedure 1, Constitutional Law 1, and another one that I don't remember—maybe Criminal Procedure. My favorite was Constitutional Law, not just because I liked the subject, but because the professor, John Valauri, was really nice and funny. He would greet each class with a cheery, "Helloooo, con law fans!" (sort of like a radio announcer bellowing, "Hello, sports fans!"). I liked my Civil Procedure professor, too—Paula Raines—who was very laid-back. Sometimes she attended the New Thought Unity® Center in Cincinnati, which I also attended. Oftentimes, she would meet me there and help me get my chair into the building.

Back then, I was so focused on Unity's beliefs in the power of thought that I did not study their views on Christianity. The organization promotes itself as a "positive, practical approach to Christianity," but views Jesus as merely a "master teacher of truths," not the divine Son of God. If I had known that, I would not have attended their services.

Even though I loved Constitutional Law, I still struggled with it. I had such difficulty understanding much of the material that I found myself reading it aloud, to myself, sometimes two, three, or four times, in my apartment or while sitting in my car in a park.

One day, while listening to music, it suddenly dawned on me: *How can I remember thousands of words to songs that are of no value to me, but I have such a hard time remembering facts related to Constitutional Law?* That led to an idea. I figured out a system to categorize cases in a way that made it easier to memorize them. I did not turn them into songs, but I developed a certain rhythm and pattern that enabled me to memorize one hundred eighty-seven case holdings.

I figured out another creative study technique that helped me. At Chase, students were allowed two absences per semester. Remember, I was taking three classes per week. Knowing how hard the final exams were going to be, I saved up my misses and then skipped all my classes for the final two weeks, during which I remained holed up in my apartment, studying ten or twelve hours a day.

My daily fast-food habit finally caught up with me that fall when I came down with a bad kidney infection. The problem was not the food itself, but the fact that I was drinking mostly soft drinks because they were easy to sip through a straw. Since I was unable to open beverage bottles, I had not been drinking enough cranberry juice, which helps fight kidney and bladder infections. As a result, I ended up in the hospital for several days. Schedule-wise, that was not a problem because I had already decided to skip the last two weeks of class. I was able to keep studying in the hospital bed, but I felt lousy, which affected my concentration.

Just as the antibiotics started to kick the infection, I received word that my Grandma Lucy, who had been in a nursing home since her mid-60s, had passed away at the age of 83. When I was a child, I had spent quite a bit of time with her, but as time went on, we saw each other less and less. We were no longer as close as we once had been, but I still felt sad. She was the first close family member that I had lost. I arrived in Dawson Springs in time for the visitation. The next day I went to the funeral at noon, ate a quick lunch, and rushed back to Northern Kentucky. I would have liked to stay longer, but with final exams looming, there wasn't time.

Despite losing my grandmother and getting sick right before finals, I ended up passing all my classes with Bs and even got a B+ in Constitutional Law. Not only did I enjoy the classes more during the first semester of my second year, but my professors allowed me to dictate my exam answers into a tape recorder, which I had not been allowed to do previously. From then on, my confidence continued to improve, and law school wasn't quite so bad.

Ron's mother visiting him in his apartment during his second year in law school.

22

THE "WOW" FACTOR

Nowadays, it's common for many universities to offer a combination law and business degree, usually called a JD/MBA, but when I started at Chase, such a degree was not available. Imagine my surprise when, near the end of my second year, I was invited to help create one.

One day, I received a note summoning me to the Dean's office. At first, I was a bit trepidatious. The last time I had been invited to the Dean's office, during my first year at law school, I received a note from a professor suggesting that I pursue a different profession. I had been doing well academically during the second year, so I did not think I was in for bad news, but I could not imagine why the Dean suddenly wanted to see me.

"Thanks for coming in, Mr. Adams," he said. "I have been impressed with your improvement since your first year. I'm hearing good things about you."

"Thank you, sir," I answered. "It's a lot of work, but I enjoy it."

"Lately, I have been talking with the head of the Business Department about working together to create a joint JD/MBA degree," he explained. "Since you graduated from Murray State with a 3.6 GPA in business, would you be willing to help us develop the curriculum for our new program?"

It was another *"You're not in Kansas anymore"* moment. Here I was, a poor kid from a small town, paralyzed from the neck down, being invited to help create a new academic program at the very law school I almost flunked out of and a professor had recommended that I quit.

"When do we start?" I asked.

The dean arranged a meeting for me with Dr. Julie Gerdsen, the head of the MBA program at NKU, and the assistant dean of the law school. The three of us went over the existing MBA and Law curricula and discussed which courses from both fields should be included in the new JD/MBA program. It felt good knowing university administrators had that kind of confidence in me.

After the program was finalized, I was invited to be the first to sign up for it. Two other law students also signed on, and we would become the first three to graduate with the new JD/MBA degree at Northern Kentucky University. NKU allowed me to transfer some of my business credit hours from Murray State, which meant that I would only have to take an additional nine hours to get the new joint degree. Before that could happen, I still had one year to go.

23

FINISHING LAW SCHOOL

During my third year at Chase, I continued to explore religion. I considered myself a Christian but was still searching for something that might improve my chances of getting healed. In the previous few years, I had seen a psychic healer and a faith healer. More recently, I had explored visualization techniques taught by Silva Mind Control and I had tried the New Thought Unity® Center. Through it all, I never stopped reading the Bible, but I still could not wrap my mind around the concept of faith moving mountains. It had been eight years since the accident and my mountain had not moved an inch. I wondered, *"Am I putting my faith in the wrong thing?"*

Since starting law school, I had stayed so busy studying that I was not constantly obsessing over my physical limitations, but my old insecurities came bubbling back to the surface when I attended my ten-year high school class reunion in early summer 1985. I had not seen most of my former classmates in all those years. I was disappointed none of the cheerleaders, who used to shout my name in front of cheering fans, showed up. Other former classmates, who had only known me as a jock, were now seeing me in a wheelchair for the first time. Some reacted uncomfortably, not knowing what to say, not realizing I was perfectly at ease discussing my condition. Others, who used to be jealous of my success in basketball, seemed to be fine, now that I was in a wheelchair, although I think they were still a bit intimidated because I was in law school and they were working in a coal mine.

In spite of certain insecurities, I had become comfortable living on my own and getting around without help. Though I was skilled with my chair, there were occasional mishaps.

One afternoon, I drove to a park a few miles from campus, where I planned to read a book. Ordinarily, after parking my car, I would release the brake on one of the wheels on my chair, which allowed me to maneuver the chair into a convenient position after pushing it out of the backseat and onto the ground. This time, however, I inadvertently released both brakes while dropping the chair to the pavement, which was on a slight incline. Before I knew what was happening, the chair started to creep downhill, very slowly, almost as if it had a mind of its own and could not decide whether to keep going or make a u-turn and come back to me. It kept rolling…rolling…rolling…finally stopping when it hit the curb at the edge of the parking lot, one hundred feet away.

I looked around, but there was nobody to help me retrieve the chair. I slid back under the steering wheel of the car, shut the door, drove to the chair (thankfully, it had not tipped over), and managed to wrestle it back into the car.

Another time I was transferring from the car to my chair, with my butt up in the air and my head tilted down when I lost control and flipped over, hitting my head on the ground and then landing flat on my back. I looked around to make sure no one had seen me fall. As nice as it might have been to have help at that moment, it also would have been embarrassing to have had witnesses to my pratfall. I managed to get back into a sitting position on the ground and struggled to get back up into the car seat. I was then able to maneuver my body into the wheelchair. The entire ordeal, from the time I fell to the ground until I was in my wheelchair, took about fifteen minutes. It was just part of life.

Though law school was getting easier, my social life was growing more complicated. By the summer of 1985, I was dating several women at the same time. I wasn't cheating; they all knew about each other. But when Jenna came along, everything changed.

Jenna and I met at a restaurant called the Ground Round in Florence, Kentucky. I had been going there a lot, as much for a certain, cute waitress as I did for the food. The waitress never gave me the time of day, but the restaurant manager, another attractive woman, always playfully flirted even though she was married, so it was never serious.

One day, the manager learned I wanted to travel to California to receive an experimental treatment to remove scar tissue from my spinal cord. The trip was going to cost $1,500, so the manager generously offered to host a fundraiser at the restaurant. *Miami Vice* was a hit TV series at the time and one of the few shows that I took time to watch regularly. Don Johnson starred as a super cool cop who wore colorful clothes that never seemed to get ruffled. On the night of the fundraiser, I dressed up like Don, complete with a white sports jacket over a sleeveless undershirt.

A corner of the restaurant was set aside for my event, but the rest of the Ground Round was open to the public. It was a busy night. Among the regular customers sitting nearby were a young woman and her mother. The daughter kept glancing in my direction, so I decided to break the ice.

"Why don't you come on over and join the party?" I asked. And that's how it started.

Jenna insisted that we go steady from the get-go. She wanted to be the only one, and I really liked her, so I agreed to see her exclusively. Before long, her mother was pushing for us to get married, but I was in no hurry. I had rushed into marriage once before, and it failed. Plus, I had enough other things to worry about, just trying to finish law school and the MBA. I was slow to respond, but Jenna's mother showered me with gifts, some of them expensive, including clothes and a gold wristwatch. Jenna's father owned a successful used-car dealership, so I'm sure her mom could afford to dazzle me, but that wasn't the issue. That first Christmas with Jenna, I received twice as many presents as anyone in her family, which made me feel very uncomfortable.

If Jenna's mom's obsession with marriage was not enough of a warning sign, something else happened that should have sent up a huge red flag.

I was making payments on a duplex in Covington, a few miles west of Northern Kentucky University and across the river from downtown Cincinnati. I started to remodel the first-floor apartment, where I was living, making it wheelchair-accessible. One day, one of Jenna's cousins was going to help us wallpaper a room, but she called at the last minute and canceled.

"Listen, Ron, I'm real sorry, but something came up and I won't be able to help you with the wallpapering today," she said.

"That's okay," I said. "Me and Jenna can take care of it."

"Great," the cousin said. "Oh, one more thing—please don't tell Jenna's mom that I canceled; just tell her you had something come up, and you canceled, okay?"

"Why's that?" I asked.

"Well, the last time she asked me to do something and I had to back out, she didn't speak to me for almost two years."

I should have known right then and there something could be wrong with Jenna's mother. I had grown up in a dysfunctional family, so my radar for that sort of trouble was usually sharp, but at that moment, I missed the warning sign. I would later come to realize when you marry someone, you also marry their family. Jenna and I finished the wallpapering by ourselves. We continued dating, eagerly anticipating my graduation and, hopefully, a happy future together.

24

GRADUATION

A law school professor said to a graduating class, "Three years ago when asked a legal question, you could answer, 'I don't know.' Now you can say with great expertise, 'It depends.'"

I still am not sure how I worked it into my busy schedule, but by the time my final year at Chase began, I had started a small construction company on the side, and within a few months, I built eight houses.

Except for that, my final year at Chase was uneventful. The classes were still hard and the study hours were long, but I had developed a routine that made the process less stressful, thanks partly to Jenna. She was a big help with studying and generally getting around. I also liked living in my own house. The commute took just a few minutes.

I graduated on May 27, 1987, with the new JD/MBA degree I helped develop a year earlier. My family was so proud. Jenna and I got married that same day. Mom and my sisters drove up for my graduation and the wedding, but not Dad. His absence came as no surprise, but I was disappointed. The wedding went smoothly, but there was no time for a honeymoon; I had to start studying for the bar exam right away.

The exam was still two and a half months off, but I was already feeling the pressure to do well. In those days, a law school graduate would get just three attempts to pass the bar in Kentucky. If I were to fail three times, I could never practice law, and all that time and money invested in law school would be wasted.

The way the bar exam was structured, there would be twelve essay questions the first day and two hundred multiple-choice questions the second day, covering twenty-one areas of law. I could have signed up for the Bar Review Class, which was sort of a refresher course covering the types of questions that were likely to be asked on the test. However, I chose the other option, called the *Nord Bar Review*, because it was self-paced and could be studied at home, using books and tapes. I figured if I took the classroom course, I would waste three hours a day getting ready in the morning, driving to and from school, mingling with friends before class, and sitting in class. By studying at home, at my own pace, I could get a lot more done. I could also study at the pool!

After moving to the duplex in Covington, I had found a used, aboveground swimming pool for sale, which a friend, Phillip Sadler, helped me install in the backyard. I met Phillip at Murray State University, where he was studying construction technology. After he graduated, we decided to start a construction company in Northern Kentucky. Until we got it going, Jenna and I agreed to let him live in our basement. That didn't last long because Jenna and Phillip did not see eye to eye on some things, and he and I parted company after we built our first house, but that's another story.

Phillip and I built a ramp for my wheelchair and a landing that was two feet below the top of the pool, which put the seat of the wheelchair at just the right level to allow me to slide into the water easily. I enjoyed floating around on a Styrofoam™ recliner, listening to audio tapes of my bar exam material playing on a tape deck beside the pool. Whenever I got hot, I could roll off the recliner, hold my breath and swim with my face in the water, using a breaststroke. (Remember, I have partial use of my arms.) Unlike most swimmers, who can turn their heads sideways to catch a breath, I could not. In the beginning, it was quite scary.

I had to swim all the way to the other side of the pool before I could lift my head out of the water. However, I eventually figured out that if I needed to catch a breath in the middle of the pool, I could tread water by reversing the breaststroke, moving my arms forward in a sweeping motion. Jenna worked at her dad's used car dealership during the day, so she was never around, but I did not think about the danger of swimming alone because I had become so comfortable with it. When it was time to get out, I would put my left hand on the floating chair and my right hand on a platform and push myself up, landing on my belly, like a beached whale, with my butt in the air and legs still in the water. A four-inch foam-rubber pad on the platform helped cushion the impact. Then, I would roll over and scoot into the wheelchair.

I studied nine hours each day for seven weeks to get ready for the bar exam. Each of the twenty-one study areas consisted of fifteen to fifty pages of detailed outlines. Each time I went through an outline, I would highlight specific areas that I understood and use a different color of ink to highlight areas that still needed work. It turned out to be a very efficient way to go through the material over and over, narrowing down the amount of time I was studying to focus on areas giving me more trouble. Eventually, I was able to condense the most important study material down to one page by the time the exam rolled around.

I took the bar exam in July at a hotel in Lexington. I was so worried about getting stuck in traffic or having an accident on the way that Jenna, her mom, and I checked into the hotel the night before.

The first day there were twelve essay questions, six before lunch and six after, each with a thirty-minute limit. Fortunately, I was allowed to dictate my answers. As in law school, the questions really were not questions—they were facts, which served as the basis for my essays explaining the legal issues involved. In each case, I pictured in my mind the relevant outline I had studied at home.

I was always especially sharp just after waking up in the morning, so both days, during my lunch break, I went back to my hotel room and took a twenty-minute catnap before hogging down a sandwich and returning for the afternoon portion of the exam.

The second-day exam was called the Multi-State Test, and it was horrific. It consisted of two hundred questions, each of which was a four-paragraph summary of a legal issue and multiple-choice answers, which were incredibly confusing, because the answer could be "A" or "B" or "C" and so on, or it could be a combination of answers. Sometimes, it seemed impossible to pick one or two answers that applied to the circumstances described in a question. There was not a specific time limit per question, but if you broke down the whole test, you had an average of one minute and eight seconds to read and answer each question.

I took my wristwatch off and set it on the table, facing me. I decided I would have to finish at least three questions every five minutes, or I would fall behind. By 3:30 in the afternoon, I was at question 183, and my brain was fried. *I'm sick to death of this,* I thought. *Who cares what the answer is, anyway?* The pressure was unbearable. I needed a five-minute break, or I would have had a mental breakdown. Finally, after relaxing a bit, I was back in the saddle. *Suck it up,* I told myself. *You've come this far. You have seventeen questions to go and another twenty-five minutes. You can do it.*

And I did.

Ron (front) celebrating his law school graduation and second wedding, which occurred on the same day. Left to right: Ruth Adams (mother), Richard Hinton (brother-in-law), Delores Hinton (sister), Ruth Waters (Richard's sister) and Joyce Boucher (sister).

25

Now, What?

I was glad to have Jenna driving the 80 miles home from Lexington. My brain was mush, and for the next two days, I did practically nothing. I felt confident about having done well on the first day of the bar exam; less so about the second day, which was probably the single most grueling test I had ever taken because of the nonstop nature of reading and figuring out so many answers in so little time, over several hours. Now, it was a matter of "hurry up and wait" to learn the test results, which would take about three or four months.

One day in October, after being away from the house for a while, I came home to find that Jenna had opened my mail.

"Guess what, Ron?" she said. "You passed!"

I couldn't believe it, even though it was right there in black and white. It was tremendously exhilarating, especially after all I had gone through—the countless hours of studying, sleepless nights, rejection, stress, and rolling myself to class through scorching heat, bitter cold, rain, sleet, and snow. *Maybe I could have been a mailman!*

Now, what? This might sound crazy, but the whole time I was in law school, I was never sure I would ever practice law, even if I graduated and passed the bar. I had gone to Chase, not because I had always wanted to be a lawyer, but because there was no real job I could get with just a bachelor's degree, without connections. Slogging it out through law school was a way to prove myself, but

I never really thought about what I would do with the degree. Having finally accomplished the goal, I had a decision to make.

I called David Massamore, the lawyer who sponsored me to be president of the Sigma Nu fraternity at Murray State and, later, had written me a letter of recommendation to get into Chase. He was still practicing in Madisonville, twenty miles from Dawson Springs. He offered me a part-time job helping him with a Workers' Comp defense contract he had with an insurance company. I did not like the idea of helping an insurance company pay injured people as little money as possible, but it was a start, and I liked David.

"Here's what we'll do," he said. "You can work in my office on Mondays, nine to five. On Tuesdays, you'll work half a day in the office and then take depositions around the state as you head back to Covington. How does $2,000 a month sound?"

That was more money than I had ever made, so of course, it sounded great. David even added my name to his firm, calling it Massamore & Adams. He thought that was funny since his previous partner had been a lawyer named Dick Adams, and the firm had been called Adams & Massamore.

It was a good way to start my legal career. Working with David allowed me to keep my house in Covington. Plus, I got to visit parts of Kentucky I had never seen. The only downside was I had to get up at 4:30 every Monday morning and drive 280 miles to Madisonville. (I was able to make it to work by 9:00 because I lived in the Eastern time zone, but Madisonville was in the Central time zone, so I gained an hour driving to work.)

Besides the work experience, what I enjoyed most about my new job was getting to spend Monday nights with Mom in Dawson Springs. Unfortunately, she was still taking care of Dad, who still lived with her and was as demanding as ever.

26

SOME THINGS NEVER CHANGE

By the time I started working for David Massamore and spending Monday nights in Dawson Springs, Dad had developed cirrhosis of the liver and was almost completely blind from years of excessive drinking. I wished he had quit years earlier because we all would have been much happier, but he loved his whiskey too much to give it up. Now, as he sat in his easy chair, listening to those awful honky-tonk records he loved so much, I wished I could feel compassion, but I only felt disgust.

Every Monday, Mom would fix my favorite dinner—roast beef with mashed potatoes and gravy (a country boy's "ice cream") and all the good stuff that went with it. One night, Dad was already sitting at the dinner table by the time I arrived and Mom was cutting up his food. I rolled up to the table and Mom started helping me as Dad dug in, hogging his own food down without waiting for anyone else. Mom had just finished cutting up my food and sat down as Dad slurped up his last bite.

"Where's my g-d napkin?" he growled.

Dad eating before everyone else could almost have been excused as a cultural quirk. Right or wrong, it was traditional in Western Kentucky, as it is in many rural areas, for men to eat before the women and children. I think that custom stemmed from the fact that, historically, men were perceived as hungrier and more deserving of food because they spent all day out in the field or at the construction site or in the coal mine, or whatever.

But when Dad cursed and demanded a napkin before Mom had even sat down—before we had even said grace—it was all I could do to keep my mouth shut. Whenever Dad barked, Mom dutifully jumped to her feet and grabbed a paper towel to wipe his face. *Why doesn't she tell him to go get his own napkin 'cause she's leaving him?* I wished.

Dad had treated Mom like dirt for years and she just always took it like a worn-out doormat. He even ran off with another woman, at least a couple of times. Once, Mom and Dad went to buy a car, and even though he was drawing $2,000 a month in pension and black lung benefits, Mom ended up making the car payments out of her paltry $250 a month in Social Security. Dad went around town bragging about how he bought Mom a new car, but the fact was he did it with *her* money! After she made the monthly payment, she had almost nothing left, while Dad still had his $2,000 to fritter on billiards, booze, and bimbos.

Ever since I had gone to work in the coal mine, and even before that, if Mom had anything nice—towels, clothes, trinkets—I was the one who bought it for her. When I was little, I remember the only towels we had were cheap, paper-thin towels that came free in boxes of laundry detergent. When I got older, I started buying Mom nice, fluffy towels, but she never used them. I would come home and all the pretty towels were neatly folded and stacked in the corner, out of reach, while the cheap ones were hanging up for people to wipe their hands on.

"Mom, why are we using these ugly towels?" I asked.

"I don't want to mess up my good ones," she replied.

It was just another example of how she did not think she deserved anything nice because of the way Dad had conditioned her.

One Monday night, while I was staying at the house, I finally had enough. Dad was being his usual, hateful self, and I snapped.

"Look, Dad, if Mom won't say it, I will. I'm tired of you talking to her this way. There's no excuse for you treating her like a second-class person. If you don't start being nice, I'll file her divorce papers and I guarantee she'll get half of whatever you're drawing, 'cause I know the law!"

Now that he was blind, Dad knew he needed Mom more than ever. Rather than face a divorce and lose half of his money, he agreed to give her three-hundred and fifty dollars a month from then on. It was the first time I had ever negotiated a legal settlement. I was only sorry it involved my parents.

27

ANOTHER ONE BITES THE DUST

The Northern Kentucky region is comprised of several counties, but the main ones are Kenton, Campbell, and Boone. If the whole area was one city, it would be the second-largest in Kentucky, after Louisville. In terms of the population density, it was a great location to start my own law practice, but it would still take time to begin attracting clients.

One of my early clients, although I did not charge him, was my father-in-law, Ronald. As a used car dealer, he was too nice. For example, when I first met him, he was in the habit of not charging his customers interest when he financed their cars. If a car needed to be repaired, he would take care of it and simply add the cost of the repairs to the loan. He also did not repossess cars when customers fell behind in their payments. It sounds simple, but I helped him understand how, by changing those self-defeating practices, he could make more money.

When Ronald decided to open a second location, we found a former motel on Dixie Highway in Florence, with a house on the premises where the former owner had lived. In return for my legal services, Ronald gave me office space in what used to be a guest room in the motel. After resolving a zoning issue with the city, my father-in-law and I moved our respective businesses into the former motel while he and his wife moved into the house next door.

Meanwhile, Jenna and I had moved into a new, twenty-five hundred square-foot ranch-style house I built with the intention of selling. The house was in Richwood, a community about seven miles south of Florence. Getting to work was easy for both of us since Jenna worked at her dad's car dealership, which is where my law office was also located. Since our schedules were different, we drove to work separately.

In the summer of 1988, just over one year after Jenna and I tied the knot, I arrived home one day. For the first time, she did not greet me with a kiss.

"Ron," she said, without any hint of emotion, "I don't want to be married anymore."

I was stunned. She could be moody sometimes, but we had never had any big fights.

"I don't understand," I said. "What's wrong? Can we talk about it?"

"There's nothing to talk about," she said. "I just want to get out and move on with my life. That's all."

I suspected it had something to do with Jenna's mom. Despite pushing us to get married in the first place, her attitude toward me had grown cooler since the wedding. I could not prove it, but I speculated my mother-in-law resented my construction company because some of her relatives, who were contractors, had supposedly been run out of Texas because of legal issues.

Jenna moved into her parents' house next to the former motel and continued working at the car dealership, which made things especially awkward since I still saw her every day when I went to the office. To her credit, she wasn't ruthless. She did not want anything from me (not that we had accumulated much wealth at that point, anyway), but the experience left me feeling bitter and hurt all over again. When Jenna and I first started dating, I had shared my belief that people change when they get married, but then I caved under pressure from her and her mom. In hindsight, I realized I should have followed my gut instinct.

28

The Practice

A courtroom is a place where Jesus Christ and Judas Iscariot would be equals, with the betting odds in favor of Judas.
—H.L. Mencken

I spent the first few months of 1988 typing my master documents—hundreds of pages—one finger at a time, in my spare time. I continued working part-time for David Massamore, which provided steady income while I was getting my own practice started, but insurance defense was not what I wanted to do. I wanted to help people, not make things more difficult for them when it came to filing insurance claims. Having come from a poor background, I figured I could help people who were at the end of their rope if I specialized in bankruptcy, family law, and workers' compensation.

Since my last name began with "A," I was lucky to have one of the first listings in the "Lawyers" section of the *Yellow Pages*. But it was not until I bought a small display ad that I finally started getting phone calls.

In most personal bankruptcy cases, the lawyer gets his total fee up front, but I would often make exceptions if someone could not afford the fee. Let's face it—most people who need to file for bankruptcy don't have a lot of money. I was willing to work out payment plans, which were not common in those days. That resulted in more business for my little law office, and soon other lawyers in my area were doing it.

One of my early clients was a young woman, about twenty years old and pregnant. She was desperate for help but had no money. I took the case anyway. She agreed to pay me later, but never did. Twenty years later, she came back to me, this time with her husband, and asked if I would represent them, even though she had not paid me the first time. I took care of her again and have since received three referrals from her. I have always believed that God rewards people who give of themselves. If you do the right thing, you might be taken advantage of, but more often than not, good things will keep coming back around.

For many people and businesses, bankruptcy is the only practical way out of a bad situation, but the laws are designed to discourage bankruptcy by making it extremely complicated. In any bankruptcy filing, there are approximately one hundred variables that need to be analyzed, including the debtor's income, investments, outstanding car and house payments, tax liabilities, and more. If a debtor has taken out a loan on his or her 401(k) plan, the timing of the loan repayment can affect the bankruptcy plan. How a bankruptcy payment plan is structured affects how much each creditor is paid and how long it will take. The nuances are enough to give anyone a migraine.

Figuring out a reasonable payment plan a judge will approve sometimes takes more time than it is worth for lawyers dealing with low-income clients or smaller cases. Early in my career, I developed a method to simplify and speed up the overall process, to provide a better result for most clients, satisfy the court and keep creditors happy. I have Bill Gates to thank for that (even though I never met him).

Nowadays, Microsoft Excel is the leading spreadsheet program in the world, but it was still relatively new when I entered the legal profession. The company introduced Excel for Mac in 1985 and a version for Windows in 1987.[10] I bought the software and designed a spreadsheet to help me calculate a viable payment schedule for any client's bankruptcy by listing almost

---

10   Walkenbach, John (December 4, 2013). "Excel Version History". *The Spreadsheet Page.*

every conceivable aspect of the client's financial picture. The software could then crunch the numbers and gave me a series of reasonable payments based on varying lengths of time in which the debt would need to be repaid.

Every variable in a bankruptcy filing is critical, no matter how small. A difference of one-tenth of one percent can mean the difference between a client's success or failure. I was not aware of any other lawyers using anything quite like my system. My system expedited cases, which meant that I was able to handle more of them in the same amount of time.

I took my system to a software developer to see if the company might want to incorporate it into their existing bankruptcy software, but they turned it down. Why, I have no idea, but perhaps I did not do a good enough job of explaining how it was better than anything on the market at that time. Now there are many bankruptcy programs available to lawyers, but I still use my own system for the most complex Chapter 13 cases because it works better!

29

KISSING COUSINS

Most lawyers like to talk about their successful cases. This is a story about one of my worst.

Early in my career, a young man and his wife showed up at my office without an appointment, insisting on seeing me immediately. I had previously met with them concerning a bankruptcy two weeks earlier, but now they were desperate to discuss something else. I told the receptionist to bring them back to my office. The wife was six months pregnant.

"Mr. Adams," the husband said, "I've got a problem with my cousin."

"What kind of problem?" I asked.

"She's fifteen years old and, well, she's been going around telling people that we had sex," he said.

"Did you?"

"No."

"Why would she say that?" I asked.

The wife sat in stone-cold silence, looking away, her lips clenched. The husband stammered.

"I guess she's, uh...she's had a really rough life and...um... she's pretty advanced for her age if you know what I mean," he said.

I was starting to get the picture. He continued.

"Well, Mr. Adams, she got mad because I wouldn't do something for her and now she's threatening to file charges against me, saying we had sex. What should I do?"

I had never handled a criminal case before—just bankruptcies, workers' comp, and divorces—but this one seemed simple. I thought for a minute what Perry Mason[11] would do and then offered my best advice.

"Here's what I think you should do," I said. "Go to the county sheriff as soon as you can and tell him your side of the story before your cousin does. That way, when she files a charge, the sheriff will already know where she's coming from, which might work in your favor. The truth is the best policy."

"Yeah, that's a good idea!" the man said. "Thanks!"

I felt pretty good about the advice I had given my client until forty minutes later, when his wife called.

"Mr. Adams," she sobbed, "we went to see the sheriff like you said, and now my husband's in jail!"

I was stunned.

"What happened?" I asked.

"He admitted he had sex with his cousin, and they arrested him and charged him with statutory rape!"

"He told me that he *didn't* have sex with her!" I said.

"Well, he lied," the wife said.

Wonderful! I thought. *My first criminal case, and I got my client thrown in jail!*

I would never have told the man to go to the sheriff if he had been honest in the first place. Still, I felt so bad about the situation that I offered to represent him for free, but under the circumstances, my hands were tied. The man got six years in prison. After he got out, he and his wife hired me to handle their divorce. I was surprised they waited so long. Instead of holding a grudge against me, the man was apologetic.

"I'm sorry I lied to you, buddy," he said.

Lesson #1: If you commit a crime, don't lie to your lawyer. Lesson #2: If you are a lawyer, don't automatically believe the first thing a client says.

---

11   Perry Mason is a fictional defense lawyer in a series of novels written by Earl Stanley Gardner and, later, a popular television series from 1957-1966.

30

CONNIE

In late fall 1989, a woman walked into my office and said she needed a divorce. Her name was Connie, and she was stunningly beautiful, smart, and funny. We were not exactly flirting, but our first conversation was as much casual as it was about business. Even so, I kept it professional because to do otherwise would have been considered unethical (even though rules against lawyers fraternizing with clients would not be formalized until years later).

I agreed to take Connie's case. She came back and paid the retainer two days later, but then she returned a few days after that to ask for it back.

"This is embarrassing, but my rent is past due," she said. "Is there any way that I might get my money back and pay you later?"

How could I say no?

Little did I know, until much later, that Connie's initial opinion of me was not entirely positive. Apparently, she was turned off by a comment that I intended to be humorous: "A woman is like a CD. When you get a new one, you play it over and over, but eventually, you get tired of listening to the same music and you want something different." I did not hear her at the time, but Connie told me later that as she walked away, she muttered to herself, "What a shame, to be such a nice guy and such a jerk."

In hindsight, I understand that my joke was sexist and insulting.

It took about six months to finalize Connie's divorce. Through all that time, we were not involved romantically, but it was clear that we liked each other a lot. Sometimes, if her appointment was near the end of the day and no other clients were coming in, she would hang around my office and shoot the breeze about anything and everything—sometimes funny, sometimes serious. Like me, she had been through many hardships. We talked a lot about how the world was changing and how we might improve things if we had the power.

Connie had two children—Joe and Rick. There were a few times when her soon-to-be-ex showed up at my office, screaming at me about all kinds of things. He was scary. I understood why she was leaving him. Once, she called to tell me that her husband was outside the apartment, pulling wires out of her car engine. I told her to call the police.

31

LAST DRIVE WITH DAD

In the spring of 1990, about a year after my divorce from Jenna, I received word that Dad had just a few weeks to live. After a lifetime resenting his alcoholism and abusiveness and him never really loving me (or at least, not showing it), I decided to try to make peace. I drove down to Dawson Springs, thinking if I was honest about how I felt, maybe he would be remorseful and apologize for his hurtful behavior. It was not to be. As I drove Dad around town, we talked substantively for the first time in a long time. To say the conversation was strained would be an understatement.

"Dad, do you remember those times when I was little that you'd come home from work every day and then you'd leave right after supper to go shoot pool?" I asked.

He paused and thought a moment before muttering, "Yeah."

"Did you ever think that sometimes me and Mom would've liked you to hang out with us instead of always going to the pool hall?"

I was hoping he would say something like, *Son, we all make mistakes. I can't undo that, but I did love y'all.* Instead, his answer was as short and cold as a glass of his favorite whiskey on the rocks: "Well, all I can say about that is I loved my friends."

I was stunned. *That's all he could say? He "loved his friends?" What about his family?* As much as I wanted to blurt out how indifferent and hurtful his response was, I kept my mouth shut.

To say anything else would have been futile. If I learned anything over the years, Dad was Dad and he was not about to change, even this close to the end. We drove back to Mom's house and I helped guide him through the door, back to his easy chair. I even turned on the radio so he could listen to that awful honky-tonk music. Then I drove home.

I returned to Dawson Springs two weeks later, a few days before Dad passed away. I was not in the room when he drew his last breath, but I was in the house. It certainly was not a happy occasion, but I felt relieved he would no longer be able to torment Mom. Knowing my father as I did, I imagine he had bragged to his friends about having a son who was a lawyer. Long before that, he had probably bragged to the guys at the pool hall about what a great basketball player I was. But why he could never show or verbalize love to the ones who needed to hear it the most will forever be a mystery.

I stayed in town until after the funeral and then drove home to Northern Kentucky, eager to get back to work.

32

FOOD COURT CONUNDRUM

One of my best friends was (and still is) Leslie Turner, an accounting professor I met while I was in law school at NKU (he later took a job teaching at Palm Beach Atlantic University in Florida). He also happens to be a quadriplegic, so we understand each other as nobody else can. Like me, he is also a huge basketball fan.

One day in April of 1990, when he was still living in Northern Kentucky, Les invited me to go with him and his girlfriend to an Indiana Pacers game. I had not been to a basketball game in a long time, so I was excited. Indianapolis is 100 miles from Cincinnati. We drove up in Les' van.

As we approached Market Square Arena (which has since been demolished), I felt a sudden, very urgent need to relieve myself. There was a shopping mall next to the arena, which seemed like it would be quicker to get to, so we parked the van and went in. Les and his girlfriend waited in the food court while I made my way to the men's room.

In the restroom, I discovered that my chair could barely fit in what passed for a handicapped stall. I mean, the stall was fine for someone with a broken leg, using crutches, but it was not big enough for a wheelchair. Nonetheless, I squeezed in and managed to pull the door shut. I awkwardly transferred to the toilet seat by pushing against the arm rests of the chair and managed to get my pants down in just the nick of time.

After I finished my business, I realized that not only could I not pull my pants up, but it was practically impossible to transfer from the toilet back to my chair. The stall was so badly designed that the grab bars were too far away for someone like me to get the leverage needed to raise a few inches off the toilet seat. I started to panic. I had visions of being arrested for indecent exposure. *"Dear Jesus, please get me off this toilet and help me pull up my pants,"* I pleaded silently.

Just then, I heard the bathroom door open and someone came in, only it wasn't Jesus, it was Les. He spoke to me through the closed stall door.

"What's taking so long, Ron, did you fall in?"

"I don't know what to do," I said. "I'm stuck on the toilet. I can't transfer to the chair and my pants are down."

Silence.

"Hmm…um…well…just keep trying," Les said. "I'll wait for you in the food court."

I heard the men's room door open and close as Les exited. I couldn't blame him. What could he do? Go ask a total stranger to help his friend pull up his pants in a bathroom stall and get onto a wheelchair? Not likely.

Great, I thought. *I'm on my own and I'm going to miss the basketball game.*

To get back into my chair, I would need to pivot counterclockwise and scoot off the toilet seat. Shoving my left hand under my thigh, I pushed against the toilet seat to lift my leg up, managing to move a couple of inches laterally. I repeated the action twice more until my right butt cheek was slightly on the chair while my left one remained on the toilet. I was more off the chair than on it. One wrong move, one slight roll of the chair, and I would fall to the nasty, urine-splattered floor. With my left hand still on the toilet seat, I stretched my right arm as far as I could and wrapped my clenched hand around the right "cane," or push handle of the chair. By pulling with my right hand, I wriggled my body until my butt was halfway on the chair. During the ordeal, I heard men come into the restroom, undoubtedly wondering what all the commotion was in the handicapped stall.

Getting back into my chair solved only half the problem. My pants and underwear were only halfway up. After much struggling, I managed to pull the front of the pants up over my lap, but my rear end and the sides of my pelvic region were still exposed. I stretched the bottom of my T-shirt down as far as possible to try to cover my bare flesh. I knew that my pants were down, but I hoped it was not so obvious to others. I rolled out to the food court, where Les and his girlfriend were drinking Cokes. I leaned in, close to Les.

"Les," I whispered, "can you tell that my pants are down?"

His eyes grew wide and his jaw dropped.

"Ron, you're naked!" he said. "We've got to get back to the van!"

We made our way out of the mall as discreetly as possible, which of course, was impossible, considering that we were two quadriplegics in wheelchairs. I stared straight ahead, avoiding eye contact with anyone, but I am sure people in the food court were gawking. It's a good thing smart phones did not exist back then, or someone would surely have shot a video and posted it online.

Les' girlfriend walked to the arena to get our tickets while Les and I climbed into the van. He sat in the driver's seat while I got in the back, down on the floor, and proceeded to make myself presentable. Over the next twenty minutes, the windows fogged up and the van shook back and forth as I struggled to get my thumbs through the belt loops and wrestle my pants up around my waist. I could just imagine what passersby must have thought was going on. The only thing missing was one of those bumper stickers with the message, *"When this van's rocking, don't come knocking."*

Finally, I got my pants up and Les and I pushed ourselves, in our chairs, into the arena. His girlfriend had saved our seats. We arrived just in time for the opening tip.

33

THIRD TIME'S A CHARM

When President George H.W. Bush signed the Americans With Disabilities Act (ADA) into law in 1990, I was thrilled. The Civil Rights Act of 1964 had made it illegal to discriminate against people with disabilities, but the ADA had more teeth. For one thing, it required employers to make "reasonable accommodations" for disabled workers and it established accessibility requirements for public spaces and commercial buildings. If such a law had existed when I graduated from law school, I might have applied to work at an established law firm. However, before the ADA passed, I knew the excuses most law firms would probably use to avoid hiring me. It was always easier to hire able-bodied employees who did not need specially designed restrooms and could get to depositions and court hearings more quickly. That was the main reason I decided to launch my own firm.

I knew the implementation of the ADA would be a slow process. Like other wheelchair users, I continued struggling to get in and out of businesses and courthouses that were not accessible.

At the Gallatin County Courthouse in Warsaw, Kentucky, the main courtroom was on the second floor, but there was no elevator. The courthouse was built in 1838 and, except for electricity and indoor plumbing, few modern improvements had been made through the years. Whenever I had a hearing, the judge, court reporter and whoever else was involved had to come downstairs to a separate room, just for me. Eventually, an attorney named Marcus Carey filed a class-action lawsuit seeking to force Gallatin County to make the courthouse ADA-compliant. I was proud to have my name added as a plaintiff, along with another disabled attorney, Tom Rouse, a county employee named Pam McIntyre, and a former county employee named Elsie Ewbank. Elsie was an amputee with one leg. In her deposition, she testified that to get to the second floor of the courthouse, she had to "scoot up the stairs on her butt lifting [her]self with [her] arms."[12] I imagined how humiliating that must have been. The county complained about how much it would cost to bring the courthouse into compliance, but the necessary renovations were finally made.

Just east of Gallatin County, the Grant County Courthouse had an elevator, but it was the old-fashioned kind, with a wrought-iron sliding gate on the inner side of a sliding door, both of which had to be opened manually, which meant that I always needed help to get in. The door was barely wide enough for my chair to fit through and the elevator was so small that, once inside, I could not turn around. When I got to the next level, if the elevator floor did not align perfectly with the hallway floor, which was almost all the time, someone would have to lift my chair up a few inches to get me out. It was especially a hassle whenever people were mingling in the hallway between the elevator and the entrances to the courtroom and the judge's chambers across the hall.

One issue that the ADA did not address adequately (and still does not, in my opinion) is the ability for disabled people, particularly those in wheelchairs, to exit the upper floors of a building during a fire when elevators cannot be used. One day, I was on the fourth floor of the Kenton County courthouse for a bankruptcy hearing when the alarm went off. While exiting the hearing room on his way to the stairwell, along with everyone else, the bankruptcy trustee, Michael L. Baker, jokingly told me, "Just wait by the elevator. It's probably a false alarm, but if it's

---

12   United States District Court, Eastern District of Kentucky, Civil Action No. 03-156-DLB Elsie Ewbank, et al Plaintiffs vs. Memorandum Opinion & Order, Gallatin County, Kentucky

not, I'll make sure your family gets a good settlement." Mike had worked with me, and we were friends, so his joke did not offend me, but it made me think seriously about how I would get out of a tall building in the event of a fire. I still don't know.

Accessibility problems do not always involve structural issues, but rather, some people simply not paying attention or not caring about disabled people's needs. I came out of the Kenton County courthouse in Covington one day to discover that a sheriff's deputy had parked illegally, so close to the driver's side of my van that I could not lower the wheelchair lift. A friendly passerby offered to back my van up a few feet so that I could lower the lift. I gave him my keys and waited in front of the vehicle. Since there was no seat at the steering wheel, the Good Samaritan had to stand, hunched over, while maneuvering the van, which might explain why he inadvertently put it into "drive" instead of "reverse." The van lurched forward and rammed my chair. Fortunately, the damage was minimal and I was not hurt.

I am always grateful for the helpful people who serve as a counterbalance to the thoughtless ones. One winter morning, following a heavy snowfall, I arrived at the Kenton County Courthouse for a hearing. The parking lot was plowed, but a pile of refrozen slush was blocked the wheelchair ramp leading to the building entrance. I was already running behind schedule because of the slow, slippery drive from home. I asked someone to please go upstairs and tell the judge why I was going to be late. About then, a maintenance worker from the courthouse showed up with a shovel and started chipping away at the ice. Within a few minutes, he had cleared a path for me to go up the ramp. Despite my being fifteen minutes late, the judge was understanding. Still, the frigid temperature, heavy traffic, icy ramp, and being late caused me to feel stressed. It was not a good way to start the day.

Meanwhile, my father's recent passing began to affect me in ways I had not anticipated. Before he died, I had never lost anyone close, except my grandmother. I did not know how I would handle someone else in the family passing. The fact that I felt nothing after Dad died began to weigh on my conscience.

Had I been too hard on him? Had I said everything that I needed to say to him at the end? Did I handle the situation the way Jesus would have?

I was still exploring my faith and attending different churches every now and then, but not on a regular basis. I thought it was not necessary to go to church to worship God, but I continued reading my Bible and other inspirational literature and listening to books on tape. I was also thinking about Connie more and more.

Now that Connie's divorce was final and no longer a conflict of interest, we started to date. Handling her case taught me one thing—I did not want to ever handle a contested divorce again. I have always considered myself a peacemaker; I hate conflict. Ever since that time, I have only handled uncontested divorces, where both parties agree on most major issues and are not interested in fighting in court.

Our first date was a picnic at a park. I wanted to impress Connie by getting on a blanket on the ground, which seemed more romantic than me sitting in my wheelchair. I assumed it would be easy since I had mastered the art of mat maneuvers years earlier at the Craig Hospital. However, unlike the floor in a rehab center, the ground was not quite level. While sliding off my chair, I misjudged the angle and did a complete head-over-heels flip, landing flat on my back on the blanket. A Hollywood stuntman could not have done better!

"Did you do that on purpose?" Connie asked.

"What do you think?" I replied.

"I think you were trying to impress me."

"Did it work?" I asked.

"No," she said as we both burst out laughing.

Another time, Connie and I went to Kings Island, an amusement park north of Cincinnati. We planned to spend the day riding rides and later that evening, we were going to see James Taylor in concert at Timber Wolf, an amphitheater inside the park. Like most amusement parks, Kings Island made special provisions for people in wheelchairs. Instead of having to wait in long lines to go on rides, there was a gate for disabled people to go straight to the front of the line. Connie and I were waiting to get on a looping, spiraling roller coaster called The Vortex when I recognized James Taylor as he climbed out of one of the coaster cars just a few feet away. I could not help myself.

"Hey, James!" I said as if we were old friends. "How was the ride?"

"Pretty wild," he responded.

"I'm Ron and this is Connie," I said. "We're huge fans. We've got tickets to your show tonight!"

He shook my hand.

"Nice to meet you. I hope you have a great time."

It did not take long for other people to realize that he was JT and start moving toward him, taking pictures and clamoring for autographs.

"Well, I've got to go now," he said, dashing away with his small entourage, trying not to be noticed.

I have always loved roller coasters, but meeting James Taylor was a bigger thrill for me than any amusement park ride. We went to his show a few hours later, and it was worth every penny I spent on the tickets.

It is not always easy for a nondisabled person to be in a relationship with a disabled one. It takes a higher degree of patience and understanding to adapt to a disabled person's physical and sometimes psychological needs. A sense of humor helps. I was fortunate Connie and I made each other laugh.

We had only been dating for a few months when I developed a urinary tract infection, which is common among quadriplegics. As my temperature reached 102 degrees, it became necessary to go to the hospital. The emergency room was crowded. After the staff pulled a curtain around me for privacy and began to care for me, Connie walked away to call her mother on the telephone. She returned a few minutes later as I was receiving an antibiotic intravenously. I still had a fever, which meant I was delirious and not thinking clearly when she proceeded to tell me about her conversation.

"Hey, Ron, do you remember I've told you about Larry, who used to be married to one of my relatives?"

"Yeah," I said.

"You know he was convicted of burglary and now he's in the Eddyville Penitentiary, right?"

"Yeah."

"Well, my mom is still friends with him and she wanted to know if she could take Rick with her to visit him," Connie said. "I told her to leave Rick with Carl." (Carl was Connie's stepfather.)

For some reason, in my feverish condition, the thought of Connie's mom driving her young grandson nearly 300 miles to visit someone in prison struck me as funny, and I began to make up a song, loosely based on "Iko Iko," a popular novelty song at that time. If the original song was nonsensical, my lyrics were even more ridiculous: *"My grandma is going to prison to see her boyfriend... Hey now, hey now, Ricko Ricko..."*

Embarrassed, Connie quickly put her hand over my mouth, but I kept turning my head away from her hand, so I could keep singing my stupid song. The doctors, nurses and other people in the ER were laughing uncontrollably.

Connie joked that I could be a successful songwriter, considering how many popular songs have been written under the influence of drugs. To this day, whenever I get a fever, especially if I am on medication, I become totally uninhibited and will begin singing. I can't help it.

As much as we made each other laugh, it did not take long for things to get serious between Connie and me. One autumn night in 1990, we were snuggling on the couch. Without saying a word, I slithered down to the floor and spun around on my knees, facing her.

"Ron, what the heck are you doing?" she asked.

"Reach in my shirt pocket," I said.

"What?"

"Just reach in my pocket," I repeated. She did.

Connie pulled out a small box, which she opened to reveal a diamond engagement ring.

"Will you marry me?" I asked.

The proposal was no great surprise. We had discussed the possibility of marriage for several months and had been looking at rings. However, she did not know that I was going to pop the question that night on the living room floor.

"Of course, I'll marry you," she answered matter-of-factly. "Now come on, you nutcase, get back on the couch."

We set a date for the following February. I felt closer to Connie than I had to anyone, but I was still apprehensive about such a commitment, especially since my other marriages had failed. I could not shake the nagging feeling that people drift apart after they get married, and then they are stuck in a bad relationship. I loved Connie and she loved me. I did not want that to change.

One of the reasons I felt so comfortable with Connie was that she came from a dysfunctional background, as I did. Even though there were still things to learn, we understood the baggage each of us brought to the relationship and had realistic expectations of what our marriage partnership would and should be like. I was not trying to make Connie into the "ideal" woman, and she accepted and appreciated me as I was. It took this relationship for me to begin to understand all the ways in which men and women are different in the way they think, feel, and communicate.

Since we had both been married before, we decided against having an elaborate wedding, opting instead for a small, private ceremony on a beach in Cancun, Mexico. I made the arrangements through the Westin Hotel in Cincinnati, which connected me to its sister hotel in Cancun. An employee in Mexico named Jerry was so helpful and made everything so easy that I asked him, by telephone, what I could do for him.

"Well, Señor Adams, if it is not too much trouble, could you perhaps bring me some CDs of Rod Stewart?" he asked.

Back then, CDs by American and British recording artists were not widely available in Mexico. I told him I would be glad to bring him some Rod Stewart CDs, which I did. Jerry was extremely *agradecido*.

Connie and I got married on the beach, at the spot where the Gulf of Mexico meets the Caribbean. The wedding went off without a hitch, except for the photographer not showing up. Fortunately, Jerry took pictures with a camera he borrowed from the hotel. For an amateur photographer, he did a terrific job.

The next day, Connie and I swam in the pool under the blazing sun and played Bingo while lounging on beach chairs. Somehow, I won five out of six games, each time receiving a free piña colada and pineapple cone as a prize.

I know what you are probably thinking—why would I drink piña coladas, considering my aversion to alcohol and all the trouble my dad's drinking had caused in the past? I don't mean to sound like I'm making excuses, but I was on my honeymoon, I wasn't driving, and the piña coladas were amazing. They were served in hollowed-out pineapples filled with pineapple juice, coconut milk, slushy ice and garnished with a pineapple wedge and maraschino cherry. They reminded me of what a pineapple-coconut milkshake would taste like if such a drink existed. Plus, since my piña coladas were free, they probably contained very little alcohol. Even after consuming five, I did not feel buzzed. *At least, not that I remember.*

It was one of the most carefree, enjoyable weeks of my life.

Ron and Connie honeymooning in Cancun, Mexico.

Unfortunately, after we returned from the honeymoon, it felt like the wheels were already coming off the marriage. We needed money, so we traded the house in Richwood for a one-bedroom condo in Covington, plus some cash. The condo was on the Ohio River, across from downtown Cincinnati. The view was spectacular, but the condo was small and not wheelchair accessible. There was a half-flight of steps leading up to the front door, so we built a ramp that was eighteen feet long and eight feet wide from the entrance to the detached garage. It was steeper than it should have been, as we soon discovered.

One day, we were going up the ramp—me wearing a suit and Connie in high heels. She was pushing from behind, while I pushed the wheels as hard as I could when suddenly her foot slipped on the wet surface. She fell and I flipped over backward, landing on top of her. It seems funny now, but it was not at the time. Connie hurt her knee and had trouble walking for several weeks.

Connie had custody of her younger son, Rick, so he lived with us. Rick's biological father, Chris, who was Connie's second ex-husband, had visitation rights with Rick once a week. Connie's older son, Joe—Rick's brother—lived with her first ex-husband, Sonny.

Shortly after Connie and I got married, Chris married a woman he had known for just one week. After each weekly visit with Chris, Rick came home to Connie and me crying because his dad had told him how hard everything was for him. Being just seven years old, Rick did not know what was going on behind the scenes, and his dad's comments were upsetting.

Divorced couples dishing dirt on each other to their kids is nothing new, but here is how screwed-up this situation really was. When Connie married her second husband, he took *her* last name. When *he* got remarried, his new wife took *his* last name, which was Connie's *maiden* name. Imagine a seven-year-old trying to figure out why his dad's new wife had his mother's former name and his mom had a new last name (mine). *It even confuses me when I think about it.*

Chris and his new wife invited Connie and me to dinner one night to talk about Rick. As awkward as the conversation might be, we figured it would at least be civil in a public place, so we agreed to meet at a restaurant.

No sooner had we ordered than Chris' new wife began telling us how wonderful she was. Everything she described about herself implied she was like Mother Teresa on steroids. She bragged about being a teacher and how much she worked and made good money and had graduated from some fancy school, and there was nothing she couldn't do, and she had two children from a previous marriage and, oh, by the way, *how would we feel about Rick coming to live with them?*

"We have already discussed it with Rick," she said. "He wants to live with us, and he'll have my two children to play with."

Connie's jaw dropped and she looked as if she was about to cry. She already had self-esteem issues stemming from a terrible marriage, and now she had just endured her ex-husband's new wife bragging about how great she was and implying what a better mom she was.

"Is that true? Did Rick really say he wants to move in with you?" Connie asked.

"Listen, Connie," Chris said, "We both want what's best for Rick. Think about it—he'll have a new brother and sister to play with. He'll still come and visit you."

"Plus, it's bound to be easier for both of you in that small condo," the new wife added condescendingly.

How nice of them to be concerned about our comfort, I thought.

The awkward conversation continued through dinner. We skipped dessert.

34

GOD TO THE RESCUE

By May, Rick had been living with his dad for about three months, but he stayed with Connie and me every other weekend. No matter how much I tried to instill confidence in her, Connie felt as if she was the world's worst mother. It was a terrible way to start a marriage. Then something really good happened. God moved in with us.

Before I met Connie and throughout the time that I was handling her divorce, I had visited several churches in Northern Kentucky just to check them out. My favorite was Florence Baptist Church in the city of Florence, just off Interstate 75, about twelve miles south of Covington. It was not what I would call a megachurch, but it was big. More importantly, the pastor, Tim Alexander, was just a great godly guy. I had enjoyed our conversations the few times I visited. Now seemed like a good time to go back.

Connie and I were hanging by a thread. I was getting tired of her being depressed and she was having a hard time dealing with my issues. We seemed to fight all the time. We even argued as we drove eighteen minutes to the church. In fact, we bickered right up until we opened the front door.

It was a Sunday morning, and there were about five hundred people in attendance, but the service had not started yet. We made our way to a pew near the front. When Brother Tim started speaking, our hearts melted. I already liked him and now Connie was feeling it. She held my hand. Tim was a brilliant speaker and what he said during that first service could have been written just for us.

We went to church every Sunday morning, Sunday night, and Wednesday night. If the church had a spaghetti supper, we were there. Connie and I still had problems to work out, but we stopped fighting and started trying to understand each other more. We were turning our focus away from ourselves and more toward God.

Florence Baptist was so different from the church in Dawson Springs, where I had gone as a teenager. Maybe the old church has changed since then, but when I went there, it felt cold and impersonal. The Florence church was warm and inviting. Total strangers reached out to Connie and me and we became friends. I could not get enough of Brother Tim's preaching and teaching. I had always thought Jesus was wonderful, but I was learning so much more than I had ever known. When we weren't in church, Connie and I studied scriptures at home and watched shows on the Trinity Broadcasting Network (TBN), filling our heads with the Word.

During the first few months Connie and I attended Florence Baptist, I kept my occupation a secret because I did not want anyone to think I was just going there to find clients. My intentions were noble, but I learned how misdirected humility can have unintended consequences. Another lawyer at the church, who many members were using, was indicted for embezzling thousands of dollars from his clients. I realized that if I had let the church know that I was a lawyer, I might have been able to prevent some people from being victimized by a dishonest one.

Around the end of July, Rick, who was now eight, surprised Connie and me by announcing he wanted to move back with us. Since we got married, Rick had gone from staying with us every other weekend to every weekend. We had been taking him to church on Sundays, and he wanted to learn more about Jesus. We bought him a copy of *Adventure Bible*, a Bible with illustrations designed especially for kids. That night, he climbed into bed between Connie and me and kept us up till four o'clock in the morning, asking questions about the Bible. I think he read the whole thing in about ten days. Rick and Connie had always been close, but it was nice to see him warming up to me, too.

Rick was starting to become something of a Bible prodigy. It got to the point where he knew more than I did about the Old Testament, which I had never studied very much. He and Brother Tim got into a little game after each Sunday morning service where they would ask each other tough questions and test each other's knowledge. All the Sunday School classes wanted Rick because if they played any games that required knowledge of the Bible, he always won. Unfortunately, even churches can have bullies, and Florence Baptist was no different. A few of the kids started picking on Rick, calling him "Bible Brain," so after about a year, he lost interest in church activities.

Connie's ex-husband, Chris, and his wife reluctantly agreed to let Rick move back with Connie and me (not that they had a choice, since Connie already had legal custody). Rick got baptized that summer and asked if he could enroll at Calvary Christian School, a private school not far from where we lived. Connie and I were thrilled. I drove Rick to school each day, with Rick jamming his heart out to Christian pop music on the radio, wearing big sunglasses, and looking cool like Will Smith in the movie *Men in Black.*

I have always had a good relationship with both of Connie's children, but I have a special bond with Rick. When Connie and I got married, her older son, Joe, was twelve and lived with his father, Sonny. Rick, on the other hand, was younger and we spent more time together, even before he moved in with us. In every sense, except biological, he is my son and I am proud to be his father. When he turned 18, he legally changed his last name to Adams, not as a show of disrespect toward his biological father, but because he felt more a part of the family Connie and I had become. Years later, Rick's "other" dad suffered a stroke and became partially paralyzed. When I went to see him in the hospital, he thanked me for how I had raised Rick. It was gratifying to realize that whatever animosity may have existed between Chris and me years earlier had vanished.

I am grateful to Connie for trusting me with Rick and for bringing him into my life early in our relationship. I hope I have made a positive difference in his life. He certainly has made one in mine.

35

Loss

Whatever problems Connie and I had during our first few months of marriage were long past by the fall of 1991. Rick was back with us and was doing well at school. Connie was happy. My law practice was thriving. I was working sixty-five to seventy hours a week and Connie worked for me, which meant we had more money. We lived modestly, but it was nice to be able to afford a couple of houses. We started building a house in the nearby community of Taylor Mill, where we planned to move. We also invested in a small fixer upper in Dawson Springs, so we would have a comfortable place to stay whenever we drove down to visit Mom and my sisters.

Everything was great until one day in 1992 when I received word that my sister, Joyce, had breast cancer. She underwent radiation and then chemotherapy for several months. No sooner had Joyce's cancer gone into remission than my other sister, Delores (Lolo), received a similar diagnosis. After her initial treatment, doctors thought Lolo's cancer had also gone into remission, but they were mistaken. In October, the cancer came back full-blown, only now it had metastasized into her bones. Lolo was told she had just a few weeks left.

Every spare moment we had, Connie and I drove to Dawson Springs to be with Lolo, Joyce, and Mom. Lolo had five grown children, who also helped care for her. She was in such pain that her doctor prescribed Dilaudid, a very powerful medication.

The night before Thanksgiving, Lolo set her alarm to wake up early in the morning. Sure enough, she got up and put a turkey in the oven, her final gesture of love for the family. We enjoyed a delicious meal, trying to keep the conversation light, even though with each bite, we knew that it would be our final holiday with Lolo.

The family had moved my old hospital bed—the one I used when I first came home from rehab in 1977—into Lolo's home, and she was now in it. A few days after Thanksgiving, Lolo was sitting up in bed. Her eyes were closed, and I could see that she was in pain. I went to her and took her hand. She knew that it was my grasp because my fingers could not grip hers. She opened her eyes and struggled to focus on me.

"I love you, Lolo," I said.

"I love you, too," she whispered.

"I know it's so hard, but we're gonna be together forever, and it won't be that long," I said.

She patted me gently on the hand and nodded. It was the last time she was able to communicate with me. Two days later, on December 2, she died.

I was out of the room when it happened. I had gone into the kitchen for just a moment when suddenly I heard everybody screaming and wailing. I knew the end was near, but now it seemed surreal. I hesitated to go back into Lolo's room because I did not know if I could handle it, but I did.

Lolo was lying in bed, her back slightly arched and her mouth frozen wide open, as if in pain. Ordinarily, such a sight would be ghastly, but a peace came over me. I do not mean this disrespectfully or to be gruesome, but she reminded me of an animal carcass on the side of the road. The Lolo that I had loved in life was no longer there. What lay in the bed was like an empty cocoon, or an abandoned seashell washed up on the beach. The real Lolo—her spirit—had left her body. She was with Jesus now.

In spite of the peace I felt, knowing I would see Lolo again, my heart was heavier than ever. Belief in a heavenly afterlife and grief over the loss of a loved one are not mutually exclusive. The

Bible says that even Jesus wept when he learned that his friend Lazarus had died.[13]

Lolo's funeral at the First Baptist Church was beautiful but seemed superficial amid such pain. I kept my eyes closed during most of the service and could hardly breathe as I struggled to maintain my composure. My son Rick, who was now nineteen, eulogized Lolo, recalling how he had first met her when he was six while Connie and I were still dating and how close they had become through the years. My mind raced as a flood of thoughts drowned out other people's words. I remembered Mom, years earlier, describing how Lolo used to rock me to sleep when I was a baby while she was pregnant with her twins. I thought about how Lolo and her husband, Richard, had bought me my first football when I was five; how I missed them when they moved to Kansas City; how they used to come to my high school basketball games after they moved back to Dawson Springs, and cheered for me. I remembered so many conversations with Lolo; her wisdom, her faith, her encouragement. She believed in God and she believed in *me*. So much more than an older sister; she was a best friend and confidant with whom I could discuss anything. The funeral director asked if I wanted a specific piece of music played during the service. I chose the song "Wind Beneath My Wings." Not the Bette Midler version, which is the most famous, but an earlier 1983 recording by Gary Morris, which I always thought was more beautiful, and so did Lolo. More than any other song, that one summed up how I felt about her. She truly was "my hero" who helped me "fly higher than an eagle."

After the funeral, Connie, the boys, and I stayed in Dawson Springs for a couple more days, doing our best to comfort my mother and my sister, Joyce. The next few weeks were hard, but Connie and I were growing closer to God more than ever. We were studying the Bible, learning as much as we could and strengthening our faith, only to have it tested again early in 1993.

In February, my sister Joyce's cancer came back, just about one year after it had gone into remission. She had been getting regular checkups, but the doctor mistakenly thought that a

---

13   John 11:35

certain small tumor was benign, when in fact, it was malignant. Having just lost her sister to the same disease, Joyce was terrified. Unlike Lolo, Joyce was determined to do anything necessary to beat it.

Joyce was hospitalized in April in Louisville, where she underwent a bone marrow transplant and more chemotherapy. Mom and my niece Lisa, who was Joyce's daughter, got a room near the hospital so they could take turns staying with Joyce twenty-four hours a day. Lisa had taken a leave of absence from her job as a police officer in Texas to be with her mom.

With Louisville just one-hundred miles southwest of Covington, it was easy for Connie and me to drive down almost every day, spend a few hours, and drive home. I thought back to the time sixteen years earlier when Joyce had stayed so many nights with me in the hospital, playing music and singing songs and scratching my nose when it itched. I wanted to be with her now.

We prayed and the doctors did everything they could think of, but Joyce succumbed to her cancer four weeks later, on May 3. I worried about how Lisa and Mom would handle it—Lisa because she was so close to Joyce, and Mom because she had lost both of her daughters in four months, not to mention having lost her husband three years earlier and her firstborn in 1933. For most parents, the memory of losing a child never goes away. Now, all Mom had left was one son with a debilitating spinal cord injury. Nobody deserved what she had endured.

36

SUNDAY SCHOOL

Losing my sisters strengthened my faith. Connie and I talked about how, if there is no God, life would be unbearable and how hopeless things must seem for nonbelievers. We read the Bible every night and continued going to Florence Baptist, where we listened intently to Brother Tim's brilliant sermons.

Connie and I were fortunate to have many friends, especially at church. One of them was a guy named Gil, who was originally from Texas but of Mexican ancestry. He stood just five feet, two inches tall, but was a hard worker, always eager to lend a helping hand. He was also a solid Christian with great faith, but he had not always been that way. He was tough. In his younger years, he had been a Navy Seal. Later, he joined the Hells Angels Motorcycle Club, and I think he spent some time boxing. Ninety-five percent of his body was covered in tattoos. I did not know what he might have done in the past, but from what I understood, he had been a bad dude. When Connie and I met him, though, he had already changed and become a born-again Christian.

One day, Gil was installing curtain rods in our condo in Covington when Connie's dad, Jim, dropped in. He lived several hours away in Indiana, but he came to visit once a week or so. Connie and her dad had not seen much of each other during her teen years after her mother left him for another man, but after Connie was grown, they rekindled their relationship. Jim was a little rough around the edges, but nice. He went to church with us a few times but showed no inclination to take Jesus seriously until he met Gil.

Gil had a great voice and he loved to sing Gospel songs. After greeting Jim and chatting briefly, Gil went back to work belting out a Jesus song while Jim watched and listened in fascination. Here was this wiry but tough-guy Latino, covered in tattoos, joyously singing about Jesus while he went about his work.

A few days later, Jim called Connie while I was at work. She told me what happened.

"That guy that was over there the other day—what's his name?" Jim asked.

"Gil," Connie said.

"Yeah. Whatever he has, I want it."

"You mean Jesus?" Connie asked.

"I need to go talk to Brother Tim," Jim said. "It won't take long."

Connie made an appointment for Jim with Brother Tim and met him at the church the next day. She waited while Jim went into the pastor's office. He came out three hours later.

"I did it," he said. "I knelt down and asked Jesus to be my Lord and Savior."

The Scripture says that when you become a new creation, all the old stuff in your life passes away.[14] That was never more true than with my father-in-law. Jim was still gruff, but he had a heart of gold and his whole demeanor changed for the better. Over the next few months, he backslid a couple of times (who hasn't?), but he was a new person.

Like most nonbelievers, Jim had long been skeptical, but seemed open to the possibility that God was real; he just wanted proof. Once, before he got saved, he asked how I knew the Bible was authentic.

"I look at this way," I said. "If you are an evolutionist and you believe two rocks hit together and created a single cell that somehow turned into the human race, okay, but where did those two rocks come from? Think about the human body and the perfection of the universe, how precisely everything works

---

14   "Therefore if any man be in Christ, he is a new creature: old things are passed away; behold, all things are become new." - 2 Corinthians 5:17

together. I think only God could have done that. Nothing goes from chaos to order."

The Bible says the Holy Spirit will tug on your heartstrings to come to Jesus, and I think that's what happened to Jim. Ever since Connie and I had been married, Jim watched our relationship grow. He had gone to church with us. He had debated the existence of God with me many times. But it took a tough-as-nails, tattoo-covered Latino-Texan whom he barely knew singing about Jesus, to give Jim that extra nudge he needed to believe. Gil did it, not by beating Jim over the head with a holier-than-thou hammer, but by simply setting an example.

***

One day, our Sunday School class was more crowded than usual. Instead of the usual fifteen or twenty, there were fifty people jammed into the room. It turned out that two teachers had quit recently, leaving just one teacher for all the adult students. There were too many people for any kind of meaningful back-and-forth discussion between teacher and students.

We really could use some help, I thought.

Then, I heard a voice. Not an audible one, but in my head. It must have been the Holy Spirit.

Why don't you volunteer? the voice asked.

I wouldn't mind helping if I was qualified, but I don't know enough about the Bible and I don't know anything about teaching Sunday School, I thought.

I'm not interested in your ability; I'm interested in your availability, the voice said. *You can do it. I'll help.*

If there is one thing a lawyer hates, it's losing an argument. I was out of excuses. God won. After class, I approached the teacher.

"It seems like the class was a little crowded today," I said. "Could you use some help? I have no skills or anything when it comes to teaching the Bible, but I do love the Lord. If you and the pastor want me to teach, I'd like to try it."

I started the following Sunday with two students—Connie and one other person whose nickname, "Holly Hallmark," was inspired by Hallmark cards because she was known for being such a giver. Soon, I was averaging thirty-one students. I loved teaching Sunday School, but it took a bigger time commitment than I anticipated. The church provided preprinted lesson plans, but I wanted to do more than just read what someone else had written, so I dug deeper into each lesson, spending ten to fifteen hours each week researching Scripture, preparing for the upcoming class. Connie helped by keeping the bulletin board updated and managing prayer requests. To do this, she posted paper crosses with prayer requests written on them, on one side of the board, and would move them to the "prayers answered" side of the board, when appropriate. It was a very clear and visible way of showing that God was answering our prayers. We were both working harder than ever, but also feeling more fulfilled.

One of the most rewarding experiences I had as a Sunday School teacher was attending a week-long retreat the Southern Baptists held at the beautiful Ridgecrest Conference Center in the Blue Ridge Mountains, a few miles east of Asheville, North Carolina. There were about 3,000 Southern Baptists there, mostly teachers, eager to share their experiences and improve their Bible-teaching techniques. It was probably the best week of my life because Connie and Rick were with me in a beautiful place, without stress. Rick had fun while Connie and I went to seminars during the day, and then we attended church services together each night. The retreat brought us closer together than we had ever been.

One of the key things I learned at Ridgecrest was that whenever a new person comes to your church, it is important to help them make at least six friends within six months, or they will leave. *Of course!* I thought. *That was one of the reasons I quit going to church in Dawson Springs when I was a teenager! Nobody befriended me!*

One of my strengths has always been caring about other people and being very outgoing. I became even more so after Ridgecrest. After returning home, I organized my Sunday School class into "care groups" of about five or six people each. Each group had a "care leader," and members were encouraged to stay in touch with each other and strengthen their friendships outside of church. We also started sending out cards to first-time visitors and casual churchgoers, inviting them back. I used to think it was possible to be a good Christian without going to church. That might be true. However, I was starting to realize, more than ever, the importance of having fellowship and worshipping with like-minded believers on a regular basis. There is strength in numbers!

"Therefore encourage one another and build one another up, just as you are doing."
—1 Thessalonians 5:11

37

THE TEN PERCENT TEST

Most people tend to put up a wall when it comes to money and churchgoers are no different. Money is personal. Many people judge your worth as a human being according to how much wealth you have, but God doesn't care how much you have; he looks at how you use it.

There is nothing inherently wrong with being rich. A lot of people mistakenly believe the Bible says money is the root of all evil when, actually, it says "the *love* of money is the root of all evil." (1 Timothy 6:10). Greed has caused countless problems since humans began trading goods thousands of years ago. When money and material possessions overtake God as the most important aspect of your life, things tend to get screwed up. Maybe that's why the Bible says more about money than it does about prayer, faith, and Hell.

At the church I used to attend as a teenager, I would occasionally drop a dollar in the offering plate because it was easy, but I never thought about God's role in my financial life until I started attending Florence Baptist. That's where I learned about tithing, the concept of giving God ten percent of everything. I'm not going to get into the nuances of tithing, such as whether it means ten percent of your gross income or net income, or whether you should donate to a church versus a charity, or whether tithing includes property you might inherit, or whatever. There are different interpretations, and whole books have been written on the subject by people who are a lot smarter than I am. However, I will tell you about my own experience.

One Sunday, Brother Tim preached an eye-opening sermon on Malachi 3:8, which says, *"Will a mere mortal rob God? Yet you rob me. But you ask, 'How are we robbing you?' In tithes and offerings."* (NIV)

I had never considered that by not tithing, I was stealing from God. Still, ten percent is a big chunk of one's income, especially for someone who is not wealthy, which Connie and I certainly were not. Surely, God would not want us to donate so much money to the church that we could not afford to pay our utility bills or buy food!

Then came the challenge. Malachi 3:10 is the one verse in the Bible that actually tells you to test God: *"Bring the whole tithe into the storehouse, that there may be food in my house. Test me in this,"* says the Lord Almighty, *"and see if I will not throw open the floodgates of heaven and pour out so much blessing that there will not be room enough to store it."* (NIV)

Ordinarily, it's not a good idea to test God. That's what Satan did when he dared Jesus to fling himself off a cliff to prove that Jesus was the son of God and therefore would not be injured. Jesus replied, *Do not put the Lord your God to the test.* (Matthew 4:7 NIV)

However, Malachi 3:10 says it's *okay to test God* when it comes to tithing. Right there, in black and white, God says to give him ten percent and *see what happens.* Connie and I decided to accept the challenge.

Over the previous couple of years, my law practice had been getting busier and busier. I needed to hire more office staff to help with all the clients, but I could not afford it. The problem was that many of my clients could not pay me because they were broke, which is why they came to see me in the first place.

In spite of our financial difficulties, Connie and I agreed to start tithing. We rearranged our household budget to set aside ten percent, which we gave to the church every week. We went to fewer movies, went out to fewer restaurants, and scaled back on shopping for new clothes. I cannot explain it, but my annual income that year jumped from approximately seventy thousand dollars to one hundred thousand dollars, which enabled me to afford to hire another assistant.

I am not saying you will become wealthy if you start tithing. I cannot guarantee you won't experience financial downturns or other hardships. (In my own life, there were certainly problems yet to come.) But when Connie and I started tithing, God really did "open the floodgates of Heaven" for us. We took the test, but he passed it.

38

JOE MOVES IN

In May of 1993, shortly after my sister Joyce passed away, I was driving Rick to school when Connie called me on my car phone with bad news about her (our) older son, who still was living with her first ex-husband, Sonny.

"Ron, I'm heading over to Children's Hospital," she said frantically. "Joe woke up this morning and couldn't use his legs. He's paralyzed!"

"What happened?" I asked, choosing my words carefully to avoid scaring Rick.

"He called me and said he got up to use the bathroom and he just couldn't walk. I called 911. He's home alone. Sonny is at work."

"I'll meet you there," I said.

I dropped Rick off at school without telling him anything about his brother. I wanted to get the facts first before causing any unnecessary alarm.

Cincinnati Children's Hospital is considered one of the best in the world, so I was confident that whatever had happened to Joe, he would receive excellent care. After the scans and X-rays and whatever other tests they did, the doctors determined Joe had suffered a spinal stroke. In all the time I spent in hospitals and rehab centers, I had never heard of such a thing, probably because spinal strokes are extremely rare. At Children's Hospital, I learned they are caused by a disruption of blood flow to the spinal cord. We were told that Joe's paralysis might be temporary or permanent. Recovery could take a long time.

Joe spent the next few months in the hospital undergoing physical therapy. Although the cause of his condition was entirely different than mine, the fact that I had been in a wheelchair for sixteen years and had not gotten better must have been discouraging to him. Nevertheless, Joe put on a brave front and Connie and I tried to keep things positive as we prayed and took turns visiting him in the hospital.

Since Connie and I were married the year before, Joe had watched our relationship grow stronger and seen how close we were with his brother. After he was released from the hospital that fall, he asked if he could move in with us. That was a mixed blessing. Connie had always wanted Joe to live with us, and I had no problem with it, but I was unsure how we could do it, logistically. We were living in a nine-hundred square-foot, one-bedroom condo, and now there would be two adults, two children, two wheelchairs, and a dog. Well, here's how we did it.

Rick had been sleeping on the hide-a-bed sofa in the living room. When Joe decided to come live with us, we got my old hospital bed—the one that my sister Delores had passed away on—and brought it up from Dawson Springs for Joe to sleep on. The boys slept in the living room and Connie and I slept in the bedroom. We made a path through the living room so when I got home from work I could get from the front door to the dinner table. There was just enough room for me to roll back from the dinner table to the bed and to the bathroom. The crowded conditions reminded me of that scene in the classic Marx Brothers comedy *A Night at the Opera*, where Groucho, Harpo, Chico, and various other people are crammed on top of each other in a tiny stateroom on a ship. If Margaret Dumont[15] had opened our front door, we all would have come tumbling out of the condo!

The transportation situation was even harder. Whenever all four of us went somewhere, we had to fit into our two-door car. It's hard enough to get one wheelchair into a car, much less

---

15   Margaret Dumont was an early 20th century actress, best known for her roles in seven Marx Brothers movies.

two. To accomplish this monumental feat, I would first transfer into the driver's seat, and then Connie would fold up the chair and put it behind me. Then, Joe would transfer into the front passenger seat, and Connie would fold his chair and put it in the trunk. Finally, Connie and Rick would squish together into the backseat, behind Joe. As uncomfortable as it was, everybody maintained their sense of humor about the situation. At least, it brought us closer together!

Despite my heavy workload, I tried to spend as much quality time with the boys as possible. One thing that we enjoyed was playing football in the parking lot outside the condo. We used a Nerf football because I could get a fairly good grip on it. Joe, who was six feet, five inches tall, still had trouble walking because of his spinal stroke a few months earlier, so he was in a wheelchair. Meanwhile, Rick, who was nine years old and just under five feet tall, would guard him. The "goal line" was the garage door at the end of the parking lot. There I was, in my wheelchair, and there was Joe, in his wheelchair. I would go, "Thirty-four, hut, hike!" and throw the football as best I could, usually off-target, but sometimes straight to Joe. Joe would push his wheelchair with his hands and use one leg to steer, making his way to the goal, while little Rick would go through the motions of guarding his brother. No doubt, the neighbors were probably peeking out their windows, thinking, "That's a damn, sad bunch of people." At least we were almost as good as our hometown Cincinnati Bengals, which in those days had a less-than-stellar record in the NFL. (I hope they know I'm just kidding. I'm still a fan!)

39

NEW HOME, NEW OFFICE

Like his brother Rick, Joe loved church and got involved with as many youth activities as possible. After being released from the hospital, he got baptized and announced that he wanted to go to Calvary Christian, the same school that Rick attended, so Connie and I enrolled him there, starting in his junior year.

Meanwhile, my law office had morphed into a large workers' comp practice. I was able to afford to buy my own office building. It wasn't big, but it was the right size for my practice. It had originally been a one-story house with a basement on a quiet side street in Erlanger, a few miles south of Covington. The front of the building was on the same level as the street, so that's where I usually parked. The staff parking lot was down a small hill behind the building, where there was a basement entrance.

I had more work than I could easily manage. I did not have enough staff, which meant that I was putting in a lot of extra hours doing administrative work. On top of that, I was driving Rick and Joe to school Monday through Friday, eighteen miles from our condo and then ten miles back to my office. After bringing them home from school, I would spend even more time preparing to teach Sunday School.

Because of my crazy schedule, I was already stressed out when I got word that Sherry, my half-sister from my father's first marriage, had been diagnosed with breast cancer. Since Dad was estranged from Sherry, I had grown up not knowing her very well and seldom having any contact with her. By the time I found out about her cancer, she had already gone through the initial treatment and at that moment, the cancer was in remission.

Sherry lived in Bristol, Tennessee, about a six-hour drive from Covington. Connie, the boys, and I drove down to see her a couple of times. It was good to connect with her, especially since I had lost my two other half-sisters, but in the fall of 1993, Sherry's cancer came back. As had happened with Joyce and Lolo, Sherry got sick quickly and passed away on November 23. Having been born just a few years before my dad met my mom, Sherry was younger than my other half-sisters. At the time she passed, she had an eight-year-old daughter. It was especially sad to see such a young child trying to cope with losing her mother.

Ron with his mom, dad and half-sister, Sherry

After Sherry died, things slowed down a bit for Connie and me, and life became more manageable at both my law practice and at home. However, one thing that remained a constant source of frustration was the tight living quarters in the condo.

I still had to navigate through a narrow path between furniture, always banging into things. It was like riding bumper cars at an amusement park, without the fun. Whenever I went to the bathroom, the entrance was so narrow that my wheels rubbed against the doorframe.

The time had come to move into a house, but it would have to be handicap-accessible, so Connie and I decided to build it ourselves from the ground up. Having owned a small construction company just out of law school (the one that I started with my friend, Phillip Sadler), I knew enough to be the general contractor. We found a good parcel of land close to our sons' school. We were able to get a construction loan and we worked with an architect to design the house exactly the way we wanted it, with wide doorways, no steps, and a wheelchair-accessible shower.

Everything was going according to plan, until it came time to begin construction. Unfortunately, the contractors were behind schedule and did not get started until late fall, which is a horrible time to begin building a house. By the time winter arrived, there was still no roof or windows to keep out the rain and snow.

Connie, the boys, and I stayed in the cramped condo that winter while the contractors continued working, as weather permitted. The house was finally finished in March of 1994, and we moved in.

For the first time in my adult life, I had a yard. As a kid, I had a small one in Uniontown, but it wasn't much to look at. Later, when Mom and I lived in St. Charles, our tiny yard was mostly weeds. In Dawson Springs, the backyard was mostly dirt. Now, in Taylor Mill, Connie and I had an honest-to-goodness lawn—front and back—big enough for the boys to play in, with lush, green grass, so beautiful that I insisted on mowing it myself. Here is how...

One of my friends from church, Wes Kidwell, and his brother Les retrofitted a riding lawnmower with a specially designed handle which enabled me to empty the grass clippings from a clamshell-style bagger behind the mower. They also built a custom-designed bracket, which attached to the back of the seat for me to lean against. Two safety straps crisscrossed over my torso to hold me on securely.

I loved the roar of the motor and the smell of fresh-cut grass because of what it represented—freedom, independence, being outdoors on my own land. About once a week, Connie helped me onto the lawnmower, using a mechanical lift and a sling, and buckled me in. Then, I would spend the next three hours riding back and forth, row after row in a straight line, carefully striping the lawn as if it were a baseball field. When the bagger got full, I would back up to the compost pile, dump the clippings and resume cutting as the neighbors watched in amazement that a quadriplegic was mowing his own lawn.

Once, while riding up a small hill, I gunned the accelerator too quickly, causing the lawnmower to jerk forward and pop a wheelie. The bagger prevented the mower from flipping over backward, but it was pretty scary for a moment. There I was, facing upward at a forty-five-degree angle, like a missile ready to launch. I shifted into reverse, which forced the front wheels back to the ground. From then on, I mowed the hill from side to side instead of up and down. Connie was still worried about me rolling over, but as with most previous challenges, I calculated the risk and focused on the reward, in this case, a beautifully mowed lawn that surely was the envy of the street! At the end of every mowing session, I would sit on my lawnmower for twenty or thirty minutes, admiring my handiwork and feeling a sense of pride in a job well done.

As a lawyer, I was used to my work taking months to get done. As a homeowner with a riding lawnmower, it was extremely satisfying to receive instant gratification. Connie and I often sat on the back deck and just gazed at the yard, thankful to have room to breathe and a beautiful place for the boys to play outdoors.

Unfortunately, the housing market was in a slump and we could not sell our condo in Covington, so we rented it out. Financially, things were harder than they had been in years, but Connie and I were happy, the boys were happy, I was working, and we were all serving God. Life was good. Until it wasn't.

40

DARK VISIONS

Driving was easy, ever since I had taken lessons at the Craig Hospital when I was twenty. Any vehicle-related difficulties that I had usually involved other motorists parking too close to me in parking lots, but whenever I was behind the wheel, I felt as comfortable as Dale Earnhardt on a racetrack. However, like the NASCAR® legend's fatal accident that would occur years later, one incident reminded me that anything can happen on the road.

There was a slight incline at the end of our street in Taylor Mill, where it intersected with Kentucky Route 16, a major north-south thoroughfare. Early one morning, while driving to work, as I accelerated to turn onto the highway, my wheelchair came unlatched from the tie-down mechanism on the floor. Suddenly, the chair slid back about a foot, away from the steering wheel. The van continued forward, at an angle, into the intersection. Quickly, I leaned down so that my torso was touching my legs, which enabled me to barely reach the handbrake under the steering wheel. The van came to a stop, straddling the center line. Had I been going straight, I might have plunged over a twenty-foot embankment on the other side of the highway. Luckily, there was not much traffic on the road at that hour. I repositioned my chair, making sure this time to lock it down, and went on my way. The experience scared me to death, but nothing like what was to come.

In June 1994, I flew to Denver for what was supposed to be a routine follow-up examination. My original rehab at the Craig Hospital in 1977 predated Magnetic Resonance Imaging (MRI) technology, and now the doctors wanted to do an MRI on my neck so they would have a baseline to help them measure future changes in my condition. The scan was performed at Swedish Medical Center, which is affiliated with, and next door to Craig Hospital. The initial results were disturbing.

"Mr. Adams, the MRI scan shows something we weren't expecting," the doctor said. "We were looking at your neck injury, but there appears to be a mass higher up in the brain."

Old realizations of my frail mortality came flooding back. Connie's jaw dropped as she looked at me, her eyes wide with fear. I had faith God would welcome me into Heaven, but I was not ready to leave this life quite yet.

"What is it?" I asked. "Is it treatable?"

"We'll know more after we do a brain MRI," the doctor said. "Can you come back tomorrow? We'd like to get you in at 5:00 a.m."

Connie and I went back to the apartment owned by the hospital for use by patients and their families. We prayed and then we went to dinner, leaving everything in God's hands. The next morning, I was back in the MRI machine before sunrise. Later that day, I got the news.

"You have an acoustic neuroma," the doctor explained. "That's a kind of tumor that grows around the auditory canal. It's usually benign, but it can cause hearing impairment and put pressure on the brain, which can be serious."

I was shocked. I had heard of people suffering headaches, dizzy spells, and passing out as a result of brain tumors, but I had experienced no such symptoms. In fact, I had been feeling perfectly fine, not realizing I was going around with a growth the size of a tennis ball at the base of my brain. I would need an operation, but the doctor said it could wait a few weeks.

Connie and I returned to Denver in August. The surgery turned out to be more dangerous than the tumor, at least, in the short term. The operation lasted eighteen hours, during which the doctors taped me to the table to prevent me from moving since they were cutting so close to my brain stem. The surgery affected my breathing, so I had to be put on a life support ventilator. When I woke up, my left shoulder was in terrible pain from having been taped down so tightly.

The worst part of recovery was hallucinating from both the anesthesia and the physical trauma where the surgeons had cut around my brain. For ten days, I lay in the hospital bed, completely out of touch with reality. Like something in a horror movie, I saw visions of dead people describing their existence in Hell, imploring me to warn the living to get right with God or risk losing him for eternity. It was utterly terrifying. Whether the apparitions were real or merely a figment of my imagination, I felt an overwhelming demonic presence in the room. I was desperate to get away from there.

On the tenth day after my surgery, Connie discreetly made reservations for us to fly home. When the hospital staff found out we were leaving, they tried to talk us out of it, but we were determined to get back to Kentucky as soon as possible. Because we were leaving against the doctor's orders, the hospital did not help us. Connie helped me into my wheelchair and we left as quickly as we could. I held a few personal possessions in my lap while outside the hospital she pushed me as hard as she could two blocks up a hill to the hospital-owned apartment where she had been staying. She threw her stuff together and called a cab. At the airport, a couple of airline crew members helped me get situated on the plane. Waiting for takeoff, I finally relaxed a bit, but still could not shake the feeling of being closer to death than ever and having been haunted by hellish visions I hoped to never see again.

41

The Case of
the Lawless Lawyer

Being a quadriplegic is bad enough but losing one's mind is worse. What I went through following brain surgery helped me to understand more clearly than ever that mental illness is real. The dead people I saw and the voices I heard were as vivid as anything I had ever experienced. I am not saying I was mentally ill, but when you see and hear things that nobody else does, it becomes your reality in the moment.

After two days back home, the hallucinations started to subside, only to be replaced by a different kind of anxiety, as the physical effects of the surgery became more evident. My left shoulder was so injured I could no longer transfer from the chair to the bed on my own. The left side of my face drooped (and still does, although it has gotten better) from facial paralysis. My speech was slurred, which it had not been before. My left nostril was paralyzed, which made me feel as though I could not breathe. I was also deaf in my left ear, and my left eye had no feeling and could not produce tears. I wished it could because for the first time in a long time, I felt like crying.

I got home from Denver on a Thursday and went to church the following Sunday. I worried how people would react to me because I thought I looked like Quasimodo[16] and spoke as if I had suffered a stroke, but everyone gave me a warm welcome. It

---

16   The title character in *The Hunchback of Notre Dame*

was good to be back among so many friends and hear Brother Tim's message of encouragement.

Unfortunately, my recent surgery and its after-effects caused something of a rift between my mom, Connie, and me. I had not told my Mom about the tumor or my operation because I did not want her to worry about me dying. In retrospect, I should have realized my total lack of communication with her for several weeks would raise a red flag, but at the time, I thought I could sneak away to Denver, have the operation and get back to normal without her knowing anything was amiss. However, with my speech now slurred and the partial paralysis in my face, Mom was sure I had suffered a stroke and Connie hid it from her. When I finally fessed up to my secret surgery, Mom was hurt and angry that I had not told her what was going on, but she quickly got over it.

Before the operation, I did not know how long it would take to recover, or if I would even survive, so I had made a deal with a young lawyer to temporarily take over my practice until I could go back to work. You would think since I was a lawyer and had an MBA, that I would have had a written contract with the other lawyer, but I did not. He was a Christian, so I assumed he could be trusted. As I soon discovered, that was not the case.

Let's say the lawyer's name was "Bob." I am not going to tell you his real name because I don't want him to sue me for slander, but I assure you the following story is true.

Bob had already been sharing office space with me for a few months. I was not charging him rent because he had recently graduated from law school and I was trying to help him get established. When it became clear I would not be able to run the office for a while, Bob agreed to manage things. Under terms of our verbal agreement, he would be free to work his own cases, but he was to give me a percentage of money earned from my own cases he handled. He was also supposed to pay me one thousand dollars per month in rent.

Two weeks after I returned from Denver, I realized I had not been receiving any checks from Bob. I stopped by the office to inquire about the money.

"Uh, yeah, Ron, unfortunately there just hasn't been much work since you took off," he said. "I mean, I've got my own clients, but there haven't been any cases involving yours because you've been away."

As strange as it might seem, I took him at his word. Then, a few days later, I needed to review some files involving a different attorney. I went to the office late one day after Bob had left. The secretary we shared was still working.

"Here you go," she said as she handed me some folders.

"How's everything been going?" I asked.

"Great," she said. "We're swamped. A lot of bankruptcies and personal injury cases. Bob brought in ten thousand dollars last week on just one case."

"Oh, really?" I said, playing ignorant. "What kind of case?"

"Personal injury. It was that one from a few months ago where the woman fell on a sidewalk," she said. "She agreed to settle for thirty thousand."

Hmmm, I thought. *It's funny Bob didn't mention that since I'm entitled to a percentage. He got the one-third contingency fee, and I should have gotten a third of that.*

I decided to invite Bob to lunch. We met at an O'Charley's restaurant near the office. After ordering food and making some small talk, I got to the point.

"So, Bob, I understand you settled that slip-and-fall case last week. Is that right?"

He looked like a deer in the headlights that had also just been caught in a leghold trap.

"Oh, uh, yeah. I forgot to mention that the other day."

"You said there hadn't been any cases, but Jenny told me you've been getting a lot of bankruptcies."

"Well, those are my cases," Bob said.

"Bob, before I went out to Denver, we agreed that you would give me a percentage," I reminded him. "You're using my office. I pay the overhead and I paid for the *Yellow Pages* ad. How come you've not been sending me my share of the money?"

I was trying really hard to give him the benefit of the doubt. I thought he might apologize for his "oversight" and offer to fix it. Instead, he just shrugged his shoulders.

"As the Bible says, charity begins at home," he said.

I glared.

"My Bible doesn't say that, and neither does yours!" I snapped. "I want you out of my building by the end of the month!"

With that, I unlocked my brakes, backed away from the table and pushed to the door with the same vigor I had used in that Louisville 10K years earlier. Did Bob follow me to the parking lot and apologize for his insulting demeanor and creative accounting? No, but I did not care. The damage was done. Our business relationship was over.

For the next two weeks, Bob and I did not communicate. I waited until he moved out before returning to the office. What I found added insult to injury. The lawless lawyer had pretty much cleaned me out. My sofa, fax machine, curtains, artwork and secretary's desk were gone—just about everything except for a conference table, four chairs and toilet paper. Fortunately, before my surgery in Denver, I had moved my personal desk and two office chairs to my home office, or I am pretty sure they would have disappeared too. Even my secretary was gone. She had recently gotten divorced and moved back with her parents, fifty miles away. I would need to start from scratch.

I bought new furniture and partnered with another attorney to run the office so I could work from home while still recuperating from brain surgery. This time, a contract spelled out the office-sharing and management agreement in detail. However, Bob's dirty work was still wreaking havoc on my business.

After reopening my office, it seemed strange that no calls were coming in since I had been paying for an expensive ad in the *Yellow Pages* for ten years, which consistently generated calls. How come, all of a sudden, the phone was silent? From home, I dialed my office number, only to have Bob's receptionist answer. That's right—Bob had commandeered my office number and transferred it to his new office! Anyone who found me in the phone book or saw the ad that I had paid for, and wanted to call me, would get Bob instead. The telephone company said there was nothing it could do since Bob had transferred the number while he was legally running my office.

You might wonder why I did not call the police to report the theft of my property, or why I did not sue Bob to recoup my share of the profits for the period during which he was managing the business. For one thing, there was no written contract, so it would have been my word against his and my allegations would be next to impossible to prove in court. Besides that, I hate confrontation. I will fight tooth and nail for a client or a child, but when it comes to my own personal disputes, I prefer to keep the peace whenever possible. In Bob's case, the amount of money and property involved would not have been worth the added stress and time it would take to fight him in court. I decided to cut my losses and move on. Bob probably knew that's how I would react. For a new lawyer, I could tell he was clever, but he was not the kind of person with whom I ever wanted to do business again.

That experience taught me two lessons. First, I learned never to enter into a business agreement without a written contract. Second, not everyone who claims to be a Christian can be trusted.

42

HUCKLEBERRY, THE LAW DOG

By 1995, two years after Joe had suffered a spinal stroke and become partially paralyzed, he was finally regaining use of his legs and could walk again, albeit with a slight limp. I loved watching him and Rick as they played in the yard with our 160 pound Saint Bernard. The dog's real name was Huckleberry, but I nicknamed him Law Dog, which was Wyatt Earp's nickname in *Tombstone*, one of my favorite movies.

Connie had surprised me with Law Dog when she brought him home as a cute little puppy from a pet store while I was recovering from brain surgery. Now, he was a big, raggedy-haired behemoth, but a wonderful companion. Fortunately, he was also a "dry mouth" variety of Saint Bernard, and therefore did not drool all over the place, except when he was eating.

One day, I had to go to the office. As usual, Law Dog accompanied me, curled up in the backseat of the van. After parking in the rear lot, I pressed the button to lower the wheelchair ramp from the van. I pivoted the chair around and got into position to roll down the ramp. However, because the parking lot was on a slight grade, the ramp came to rest at an awkward angle on the pavement, which caused the chair to roll crooked and become jammed at a 45-degree angle near the bottom. One wheel was shoved against one edge of the ramp, with the other wheel squeezed against the opposite edge. I could not roll down, nor could I back up to reposition the chair. I was stuck.

"Now what am I gonna do?" I thought.

I did not have a cell phone, as they were not in common use at that time, so there was no way to call for help. Plus, it was a weekend, which meant my family would not have a reason to miss me right away. The only thing I could think of was to make myself fall forward onto the ground. It did not seem all that dangerous. The pavement was just thirty inches below. If I could get safely onto the ground, I thought that someone would eventually find me.

I analyzed the desired trajectory and scanned the ground to make sure I would not land on broken glass, a nail, or some other object that might cut me. I cautiously leaned forward and pushed with my arms, launched my body from the wheelchair and landed with a THUD on the blacktop. I managed to cushion the impact with my arms so that my face did not hit the ground. Now I was lying face-down, just a few inches from the basement entrance, but unable to get to it.

"Help!" I shouted. "Help! Help!"

Nobody heard me, except Law Dog. My shaggy best friend sauntered out of the van to get a closer look, which, for an instant, gave me reason to hope. Now, if Law Dog had been more like Lassie or Rin Tin Tin, this is the point of the show where he would have gone for help. I imagined it going something like this:

Law Dog: Ruff ruff ruff!

Sheriff: What is it, fella?

Law Dog: Ruff ruff!

Sheriff: What's that? You say there's a lawyer lying on the ground, with the sun beating down on him and nothing to drink?

Law Dog: Ruff!

Sheriff: Show me where! Let's go!

But of course, it was nothing like that. Instead, Law Dog sniffed me, licked my face, climbed back into the van, and laid down in the backseat.

I yelled for help again, but then realized that being stressed was not going to solve anything, so I might as well relax. I heard an occasional car drive by, but motorists could not see me from the street. However, a pedestrian walking on the sidewalk would be able to look down the hill. Twenty minutes later, that's what happened.

"Sir! Are you okay?" someone asked.

A man came down the hill, but as he got close, my trusty guard dog suddenly sprang into action, leaping from the van, snarling and barking as if he was getting ready to devour the poor man alive. Law Dog was huge—over five feet long—and when standing on his hind legs, could be terrifying. The man looked as if he was about to soil himself.

"Get down, Huck!" I yelled. "This man is helping me!"

Law Dog backed off. After regaining his composure, the stranger helped me get up off the ground and into my chair. I never found out if he had to change his underwear, but I wouldn't be surprised.

Law Dog was more than a service dog; he had a way of comforting my clients, many of whom came to see me under the most difficult circumstances. Most of the time, he sported one of my red, white, and blue neckties, which hung down almost to the floor whenever he stood on all fours. Oftentimes, people would sit in my office and pet Law Dog during a consultation. Once, a young woman brought her grandmother in to discuss her will and estate planning issues. Instead of sitting in a chair, the granddaughter sat on the floor and gently held Law Dog's paw as if it were a child's hand.

The end came for Law Dog when he was eleven. Connie and I made the hard decision to euthanize him because arthritis in his legs had become so painful and untreatable. Law Dog was smart, compassionate, protective, and loyal. If he had been human, I would have made him a partner.

43

THE GOVERNMENT
BREAKS THE LAW

In 1999, a new federal courthouse opened on Fifth Street in Covington, Kentucky. The former federal courthouse, a few blocks away, had been built in 1946 and was far from ADA-compliant, so I eagerly anticipated the handicap-accessible amenities that I imagined the new building would have.

The first day I arrived for a bankruptcy hearing at the new courthouse, I was stunned to discover there were no handicap parking spaces on the street. As I drove around the building, it appeared there were just two handicap spaces in the adjoining fenced-in parking lot, which was reserved for judges and courthouse staff but not for attorneys or other visitors. The only place where there was enough room to get my wheelchair out of the van was a no-parking zone in an alley, so that's where I parked. I put my emergency flashers on and entered the building through a side door. As I went through the metal detectors, I spoke to one of the U.S. marshals in charge of security.

"Just so you guys know, that's my van outside with the flashers on," I said. "I can't believe there aren't any handicap parking spots outside the courthouse."

"You're kidding," the marshal said. "I didn't know that. I'll bring it up with the Office of Facilities Management. Why don't you park in the alley, for now? We'll make a note of it."

It surprised me that the government was breaking its own law by having a new building that was not ADA-compliant. If it had been a private business, the owner could face a hefty fine, but when it comes to the government, rules don't always apply.

I parked in the alley for several months and never got a ticket. True to their word, the U.S. marshals kept an eye on my van, but they could not watch it every minute. One day I came out to find that my van had been sideswiped. I went back inside to tell the marshals. Nobody had reported the accident; it was a hit-and-run. The marshals called the Covington police. They said they would check the video from the surveillance cameras in the alley. By the time I got back to my office, the police and the marshals had already solved the case. They called to tell me the culprit was a cable TV van. The company's insurance adjuster came to my office the next day and was happy to pay to repair my van. The driver was not charged, even though he committed a crime, and I did not get a ticket, even though I was parked illegally. Everyone was happy, except now I had no place to park.

It had been eight months since I reported the parking problem, and nothing had been done. The marshals offered to let me park in the secured parking area. We agreed on a plan whereby I would call them on my cell phone ahead of time, and someone would open the gate. That was fine with me, but it did not solve the overall lack of parking for other disabled motorists who had court business.

Coincidentally, the new Kenton County Justice Center, a few blocks from the federal courthouse, also was non-ADA-compliant. There were only a couple of handicap spaces in the adjoining parking garage, but to get from the garage into the courthouse, a person in a wheelchair would have to go down in an elevator to the street level, and then push about a block on the sidewalk to the public entrance, where there was no wheelchair ramp. Instead of a ramp, there was a chintzy little wheelchair porch lift. Anyone needing to use it would have to wait for a security guard to come out with a key to turn it on just to go up a half-flight of stairs.

One day I received a call from a reporter named Peggy Kreimer, who was working on a story for the *Kentucky Post* about courthouses being inaccessible to wheelchairs.[17] Someone had given her my name. I was more than happy to discuss the obstacles I had encountered. After the story ran, things started happening. Very quickly, handicapped parking spaces appeared outside the federal courthouse. A few months later, the Kenton County Justice Center replaced the cheap little porch lift, which probably had cost about $4,000, with an elevator that cost $170,000 to carry wheelchairs up a half-flight of steps. The new elevator was already being planned before the newspaper article ran, but the story helped shed light on a problem that affected many disabled people who needed to use those courthouses. It would have been a lot cheaper and easier to build a wheelchair ramp in the first place, but the government does not always do what makes the most sense.

Courtesy the E.W. Scripps Company

---

17 Peggy Kreimer, "A trial by wheelchair," *The Kentucky Post*, July 15, 2000, pages 1 and 7K.

44

A NEW ANGEL

Mom had always had health problems, but as she grew older, there were more of them, with greater frequency and increasing severity. In 1985, when she was 67, she underwent a quadruple bypass operation, which went well, but ten years later, she developed congestive heart failure, probably due to a lifetime of smoking. The congestive heart failure caused fluid to build up throughout her body, including her lungs, making it hard to breathe. The first year of her diagnosis, she was hospitalized and placed on a ventilator five times. The doctor treated her with potassium and Lasix, a kind of loop diuretic, or water pill, to help her body get rid of excess water and salt. Each time, after receiving treatment, the swelling went down, Mom's breathing improved, and she went home.[18]

From talking with the doctor, I learned that if we could keep the fluid from building up in the first place, Mom could avoid the whole downhill process that caused her to be hospitalized. The key was recognizing the symptoms before it was too late. By measuring Mom's abdomen and weighing her every hour, it was possible to see if she was starting to get worse because her waist would be about a half-inch bigger and she would gain two or three pounds per hour. When that happened, she could be given potassium and Lasix to reverse the fluid build-up. Since I lived 250 miles away, the regular weighing and measuring were left up to her professional caregiver at home.

18   Individual treatments and results may vary. Follow your doctor's advice.

"Mom, you know I love you and I'm doing everything I can to make things better for you," I told her.

"I know you are, Ronnie," she said.

Connie and I drove to Dawson Springs to see Mom on weekends, but the caregiver looked after her on most other days and made sure she got her medicine when needed. After we started monitoring her weight and waist size regularly, she did not require hospitalization for about a year.

In 2000, when she was eighty-two, Mom decided to move in with my cousin, Phyllis, a licensed practical nurse (LPN) who lived fifty miles to the north in Henderson County. One night, Mom had trouble breathing, and Phyllis dialed 911. The ambulance took her to the nearest hospital, which was in Henderson, instead of her regular hospital in Madisonville. I could not drive down for a couple of days, but I assumed Mom would receive decent care. I was wrong.

When Connie and I arrived at the hospital on Friday night, Mom's face and body were swollen and fluid was leaking through the pores in her legs, a common symptom of congestive heart failure. It would have been obvious to any first-year medical student that fluid was building up in Mom's body, but for some reason, the hospital had not given her the proper medication. On top of that, the nurse informed us that Mom had developed a staph infection.

"The doctor thinks her lungs are too dry for Lasix," she said.

"How can they be too dry when there's water leaking out of her legs and she's all swelled up?" I asked. The nurse could not explain.

"When will the doctor be in?" I demanded. "Tomorrow," the nurse said.

I got a piece of paper and with Connie's help, wrote some questions and put them in my Mom's file, right on top of the other documents, so the doctor could not miss them. Mom was sleeping. Connie and I left the hospital and checked into a hotel.

I expected the doctor to call first thing in the morning, but he did not. Connie and I returned to the hospital just before noon. Mom's face was bulging like a chipmunk with a mouthful of acorns and her legs were as big as tree trunks. She was getting worse by the hour. *Where is the doctor? Who is in charge? I thought.*

I finally got the attention of the head nurse and asked if we could speak privately. We went to another room and closed the door.

"I don't understand what's going on here," I said. "Has the doctor been here yet?"

"Yes, he came in this morning," the nurse said.

"Did he look at my mom's chart? Did he see my questions?"

"I think so."

"Well, why didn't he call me?" I asked. "I left a note!"

"I'm sorry, Mr. Adams, I don't know."

"This situation with my mom is nothing new," I said. "She's going downhill by the hour. We have avoided these issues for years by giving her potassium and Lasix. It works every time."

"All I can tell you is that the doctor doesn't think she needs Lasix."

My blood pressure was rising.

"Ma'am, I'm a lawyer, and I've been around hospitals my whole life," I said. "That woman in there is my mother, and y'all are killing her. If she dies, I'm gonna own a piece of this hospital!"

I had never threatened to sue anyone before (except on behalf of clients), but I was angrier than ever. I asked the nurse to call the doctor and have him call me back. Connie and I waited. Three hours later, we were still waiting. Finally, I called Madisonville Regional Hospital and asked for Mom's regular physician, Dr. Craig Admundson. Even though he was off duty, it took him just fifteen minutes to call me from a golf course.

"Mr. Adams, it's good to hear from you," he said. "How can I help you?"

I brought him up to speed regarding my mom's situation.

"She can hardly breathe, and I can't get the other doctor to talk to me," I explained. "It looks like the same issue that you've been treating for years with potassium and Lasix. Would you be willing to call the other doctor? I'd rather move her to Madisonville than keep her here in Henderson and die."

Twenty minutes later, Dr. Admundson called back.

"The other doctor and I disagree on your mother's treatment, but he's willing to let you move her to Madisonville if you sign a waiver assuming all liability," Dr. Admundson said. "She could die during transport."

"She's already dying at that hospital!" I said. "I'm trying to save her!"

Within minutes, Dr. Admundson had arranged the transfer. Connie and I followed the ambulance from Henderson to Madisonville, about twenty-five minutes away. By the time we parked the car and made our way to the ER, Mom was already receiving Lasix intravenously, thanks to Dr. Admundson having ordered it. Fifteen minutes later, the hospital staff had drained 1000 cc of urine from Mom, the swelling was down, and she was breathing more easily. The next day, she was back to almost normal and ready to return home with Phyllis.

For the next two months, I drove to Phyllis' house every Friday and back home on Sunday night. A few times, I took Mom shopping and out to dinner. She was better than she had been in the hospital in Henderson, but I think those three days of inadequate care when she was filled with fluid and struggling to breathe and not receiving the proper medication had taken a toll. She was never quite the same. The experience was a stark reminder that not all medical professionals are equally competent or caring, and even those who are can make mistakes. When it comes to medical care, never be afraid to ask questions and insist on another opinion if something does not seem right, especially when dealing with a potentially life-threatening condition.

One Friday, while I was getting ready to drive down, Phyllis called to tell me that Mom was having a harder time breathing than usual. I drove straight through without stopping. By the time I got there, Mom was unconscious and barely breathing. I positioned my wheelchair so that my knees touched the mattress and leaned forward so that my head was on her pillow. I could tell that she was suffering. I stroked her forehead.

"Hey, Mom, if you can hear me, I just want you to know I love you," I whispered. "It's all right if you want to go be with the

Lord. You do whatever you need to do. I'll be okay and we'll see each other again soon."

I have always heard that people who are in a coma are often aware of their surroundings and can understand what people are saying. I believe it because, at that moment, Mom moved her cheek against my face slightly, as if snuggling. She could not speak, but I knew that she heard me. She passed in her sleep, three hours later.

In high school, I had to write an essay about the most successful person I knew and I picked Mom. She only had a third-grade education, and she worked hard back in the day when women didn't get paid much, but she managed to raise a family and she instilled good values in us, in spite of many hardships. She meant everything to me, but when she passed, I felt okay. Having lost three sisters and my dad within a short period, I had become accustomed to dealing with death. Toward the end, Mom had no quality of life. I think she was hanging on, just to see me one more time, but even that became too much of a struggle.

I stayed in Dawson Springs for a couple of days, and Connie drove down for the funeral with friends. It was a beautiful service. Our son, Rick, gave the eulogy, as he had done for Lolo a few years earlier. We buried Mom next to Delores, Joyce, and Mary Lou, Mom's first daughter, who had died as an infant in 1933.

I thought back to when I was a child when the Jehovah's Witnesses predicted that the end of the world was coming soon and how, instead of being scared, I was excited to know that a time was coming when I could be with Mom and she wouldn't have to be sick anymore, and we could both be happy. I am still looking forward to that day.

45

WORKING AT
THE CARWASH

I spent the next three years rebuilding my practice and working with a speech therapist. My speech improved, but I still talked more slowly than I had before the brain surgery. The facial paralysis diminished, but the doctors informed me that it would most likely be permanent to some extent. I went into the office to meet with clients as needed, but worked mostly from home while my new partner handled the day-to-day operations. Two years after parting company with Bob, the former partner who ripped me off, I was finally also able to get my original phone number back after he let it go.

Working at home gave me the freedom to home-school our younger son, Rick. Connie and I felt that he was not getting the education he needed at the private Christian school that he was attending, so we took him out. Many Christian schools are excellent, of course, but this particular one did not have the high academic standards that we expected, considering the tuition we had been paying.

I also signed up for a personal development course from Zig Ziglar, the legendary motivational speaker and author. Fifteen years earlier, I had studied several of Tony Robbins' motivational books. He was great, but what I especially liked about Zig Ziglar was that so much of his positive-thinking techniques were based on Biblical teachings. Whenever I was driving in the car, I would listen to a Zig Ziglar tape or CD.

I never met Zig, but he helped me in many ways, especially when it came to my next medical challenge. Although I had been a quadriplegic for twenty-two years, I always had partial use of my arms, but in 1999 I began to experience a loss of coordination in my left arm. I returned to the Craig Hospital in Denver, where the doctors discovered scar tissue growing in my spinal canal. I would need another operation to remove the scar tissue, or it would probably keep spreading up my spine and affect my ability to breathe. I also needed to have the vertebrae in my neck fused again.

Due to an infection, I was in the hospital for twenty days. Each day, the staff put my feet on the floor so that I could sit up for twenty minutes on the side of the bed. That might not sound like much, but it's important because lying prone for twenty-four hours straight can cause other medical problems.

After the spinal fusion, I had to wear a cervical collar around my neck for ninety days, which meant that I could not work or do much of anything else. It was close to Christmas when I returned home from Denver. All the Christmas music, TV specials, and commercials were a constant reminder that I did not have much money. But for some reason, Zig Ziglar's words of wisdom and business strategies kept me in a positive mood, always looking forward, not backward, believing that I could accomplish anything. As much as I enjoyed being a lawyer, the time had come to expand my professional horizons.

I used to get my car washed at least once a week at a place near my office. The carwash manager, Danny, didn't have much schooling, but he was really smart and strong as a horse. One day, he showed me the numbers.

"This place is a gold mine, Ron," he said. "You should buy your own carwash. I could run it for you."

After talking it over, Connie and I decided to follow Danny's advice, except instead of buying an existing carwash, we would build a new one from the ground up, which would also offer oil changes. We borrowed money, pledging every asset we owned—

my little office building, our little house, my late mother's house (the one that I had bought and my brother-in-law rehabbed years earlier), and more. My Uncle David even chipped in thirty thousand dollars.

We decided to give our carwash a NASCAR™-inspired name—*Fantastic Finish*—because racing was popular. A gas station convenience store called Speedway had recently opened nearby, and the owners of the Kentucky Speedway, a racetrack forty miles away, were trying to get NASCAR™ to come there. I could hardly wait for Fantastic Finish to open and the money to start rolling in. There were just two problems—we had picked a terrible location, and then terrorists attacked the United States.

46

9/11 and Beyond

On September 11, 2001, I was in divorce court in Covington for an early morning hearing, at the time the first plane flew into the North Tower of the World Trade Center in New York City. After I left the courthouse at 9:00 a.m., I was not listening to the radio, so I did not learn of the attack until I arrived back at the office. By that time, the second plane had hit. My staff was talking about how the country was under attack. The Internet was still new back then, and we did not have it in the office, but we had a TV. Watching those horrible images made me angry, as I tried to imagine how anyone but Satan himself could be so evil.

"Be careful," I warned my staff. "Whoever is doing this might be monitoring phone calls."

That might seem overly paranoid now, but at that moment, nobody knew who was behind the attack or what high-tech resources they might have. For all I knew, our office was bugged.

"You think you've done something brave and mighty, but you're nothing but cowards!" I announced loudly, in case spies or terrorists were listening. "You killed innocent women and children! My name is Ron Adams, and this is my office, so come and get me, you chicken-shits!"

My staff was speechless. They thought I was crazy, but they understood. Everyone was in shock. I went home and got my late father's World War II American flag out of a drawer. It was one of the few things I ever got from him that made me proud, and if ever there was a day for American pride and patriotism, this was it. I returned to the office and had my staff hang the flag. It took up most of the wall.

I was filled with rage toward the terrorists. The truth is that if we are really where we should be spiritually, we would pray for those who persecute us and *turn the other cheek,* as Jesus said. But I hated them. Did that mean I was not a Christian? Of course not! It meant that I was human, which includes being hypocritical at times. I still don't have everything figured out and probably never will. The Bible says that David, who was Israel's greatest king, was a man "after God's own heart." I am sure that if terrorists had done to the people of Israel what they did to New York City, David would have gone out and mopped up the desert with them, as he did to the Amelekites.[19] However, since I was not in a position of power, I would leave vengeance up to God. And, of course, Uncle Sam.

Meanwhile, life would go on. Americans needed to show the world we were not going to let terrorists intimidate us. President George W. Bush urged everyone to return to work and to "work hard like you always have." With that in mind, construction on the carwash continued through the fall and winter, as Connie and I looked forward to a grand opening in the spring of 2002.

True to my word, I hired Danny to manage Fantastic Finish and even gave him partial ownership. On opening day, we had a big celebration. Race fans and people with dirty cars came from everywhere to experience the area's first NASCAR™-themed car wash, complete with a black and white checkered-flag floor, racing memorabilia in the lobby, and different levels of car washes with names like "The Daytona 500" (the works) and "The Talladega." Kids loved it. That first day, we did about one hundred and fifty car washes and thirty oil changes. It seemed that we were really onto something. Until we weren't.

Like a Ferrari with a flat tire, Fantastic Finish took off with a roar, but did not get far. The economy tanked after 9/11 and people started cutting back on unnecessary expenditures. Let's face it—it's cheaper to wash your own car than take it to a

---

19   1 Samuel 30:1-20 (…David fought them from dusk until the evening of the next day…)

commercial carwash. The other problem was the location, just off I-275 at the Route 9 exit in Wilder, Kentucky. When I bought the land, I thought it would be a good spot, so close to Northern Kentucky University. What I failed to consider was the fact that, A) Most college students are in too big a hurry or too broke to get their car washed on the way to class, and B) There was nothing else at that highway exit to attract motorists, except for a soccer field and a Dairy Queen.

I tried to negotiate a cross-promotion with the owner of the soccer complex to offer parents a discount to drop their car off and have it washed while they were watching their kids' games, but not enough parents cared. After three years, Fantastic Finish failed to live up to its name. I decided to cut my losses and close the business, for which I still owed the bank one million dollars. Up to our eyeballs in debt, Connie and I were forced to declare bankruptcy, the irony of which was not lost on me. Adding insult to injury, the bank foreclosed on my office building, which I had put up as collateral. I would have to borrow money to buy my own building back if I wanted to continue practicing law at that location, which I did.

47

Nearly Contemptible

I am blessed to get along with most lawyers and judges. Most people in the legal profession will treat you with respect if you act professional and show up on time, but sometimes things do not go according to plan.

I had a Chapter 13 bankruptcy hearing scheduled in Frankfort, Kentucky, the state capital, an hour-and-a-half from home. The hearing was to be in front of Trustee Beverly Burden, a former assistant attorney general for the Commonwealth of Kentucky who had a no-nonsense, by-the-book reputation. I had never met her, nor had I ever been to the building where the hearing was to take place. After fighting traffic, finding a place to park, and pushing my wheelchair three-hundred feet to the main entrance, I was running a few minutes late. Once inside the building, it still took a few minutes to find the hearing room, so by the time I got there, I was plenty stressed and not thinking clearly. Trustee Burden was already seated at the bench when I rolled through the door and blurted out something that I immediately regretted.

"Sorry I'm late, Hon."

The room temperature dropped fifty degrees. If there had been a trap door beneath me, I would have gladly disappeared through it.

"What did you call me?" she asked.

Oh, my God, what did I just do? I thought.

Please understand I have the utmost respect for judges and trustees regardless of their gender, but back then (in the early 2000s), there were not many women in those positions in Kentucky and I had never argued a case before one. Calling a woman "hon" is common in the South and is not necessarily meant as a sexist pejorative. In fact, it is usually meant as a courteous term, like "ma'am" or "sir," although certainly not in a professional setting.

"Your Honor," I said, "I apologize for saying that. It's a habit. I grew up in a small town and that's what my mama called other women and that's how she taught me to talk. I didn't mean any disrespect."

Trustee Burden stared at me for a moment and said nothing more about my offhand remark and then proceeded with the hearing. I was lucky she did not put me on a blacklist.

And then there was the time I had a brief, very awkward moment with Judge William S. Howard, a United States bankruptcy judge in the Eastern District of Kentucky. By the early 2000s, I had argued hundreds of cases in front of him and never had a problem until…

One morning, I had the first case on the docket, which meant the courtroom was full of other lawyers and clients waiting for their cases to be called. When mine was called, I pushed my wheelchair up to the podium.

"Ron Adams on behalf of the debtor," I began.

Judge Howard interrupted.

"Counselor, where is your jacket?" he asked sternly.

"Excuse me?"

"Local rules require you to wear a suit coat in court," he said.

It is true that I was not wearing a suit coat, but I had never worn one, although I always wore a tie and a starched, white dress shirt. The judge had seen me dressed like this many times before and had never complained. However, it would be a mistake to argue with him now. All I could do was answer his question respectfully and honestly.

"Your Honor, I don't wear a suit coat because it gets in the way when I transfer in and out of my car and when I'm pushing my wheelchair two or three blocks to the courthouse," I explained. "I can't do that with a suit coat on."

A hush fell over the courtroom. The hair on the back of my neck stood up and my heart pounded as the judge just sat there, looking down at the computer on his bench, avoiding eye contact. *What is he thinking?* I wondered. *Am I going to be held in contempt of court?* I had never been held in contempt, and I certainly did not want the first time to be because of how I was dressed. After about twenty extremely uncomfortable seconds, I broke the silence.

"Well, Your Honor, at least I'm wearing a really great tie."

The courtroom erupted in laughter. Even Judge Howard seemed amused.

"Okay, Mr. Adams," he said, smiling. "Proceed."

I am happy to say that the judge ruled in my client's favor.

Until he retired in 2009, I argued many more cases in front of Judge Howard and he never brought up my casual attire again. However, plenty of my colleagues did. From then on, when I passed them in the courthouse, some lawyers would razz me with, "Hey, Counselor, where's your jacket?"

I ran into Judge Howard at a professional conference a couple of years later and introduced him to Connie. He could not have been friendlier. I do not know why he admonished me that one time, but he was probably just having a bad day. We all do.

48

POOR, POOR, PITIFUL ME

The carwash debacle and the economic downturn that followed 9/11 were starting to put a strain on my marriage. Financial stress is at the root of many divorces and that was a very scary thought. I did not want to lose Connie, but we were bickering more because money was coming in less, even though I was putting in upwards of eighty hours a week at work. With staff salaries and the mortgage payments on the house and my little office building and now the failed carwash, I was on the hook for $16,000 per month. Something had to go. I would love to have gotten rid of the carwash, but nobody in their right mind would buy it. It would have made no sense to fire my staff and sell the office building because I needed to keep working. Connie and I made the tough choice to sell our house and move into the basement of the law office toward the end of 2005.

I started feeling sorry for myself all over again. *Why me, God?* I asked, repeatedly. *I'm not a bad person. Why do I have to lose everything? Why do bad things keep happening?*

I tried to stay focused on positive messages from motivational preachers and authors like Joyce Meyer, Mark Hankins, and Creflo Dollar. Then I remembered an analogy I had heard about, years earlier, involving a mountain—*If you keep going around the same mountain, eventually you will wear a trench at the bottom.*

I had been around that mountain so often I felt I would pass out if I had to do it one more time. But how to stop? That was the million-dollar question, and I didn't have a million dollars. I was so used to losing I did not know how to stop making the same mistakes over and over. *Why wouldn't God help me? Hadn't I suffered enough?* Then, the Holy Spirit spoke to me. I don't mean that I heard an actual, audible voice, but the message was as clear and bright as a flashing neon sign—*It's not about me, Ron. It's about you.*

What did that mean? How could it be about me? I had tried everything I knew to do, and nothing worked. I was sick to death of bad luck. I had spent years struggling and trying to help others and working hard and praying and working even more and going to church, and in spite of occasional successes, I…was…still… getting…nowhere. My whole life had been one step forward and two steps back. I wasn't just going around the mountain; I was trying to climb over it, but each time I got near the summit, I slipped back down.

It's about you baffled me for a couple of days. I began to wonder if it was really God speaking, or just a crazy thought I could not get rid of, sort of like a catchy song that gets stuck in your head. I admit I had not really listened much to the Holy Spirit for most of my life, but this message was too intense to be anything else.

All of a sudden, I had a revelation. It really was more about me than God! I had always thought of myself subconsciously as not good enough, but the Holy Spirit was saying I have the strength, with God's help, to change my circumstances and even my destiny. Maybe not to heal myself, but to climb out and *stay out* of the muddy pit that I kept falling into. It was not enough that I was working hard and trying to do the right things—I needed to change my way of thinking. Again.

Positive thinking was nothing new to me. I had practiced such philosophies or strategies before. I had listened to tapes by motivational guru Tony Robbins. I had read books by the great Zig Ziglar. During law school, I had taken Silva Mind Control courses and practiced the "mirror technique," standing in front of a mirror and verbalizing positive thoughts about myself or affirmations. What I needed were *declarations*.

In the context of positive thinking, the difference between an affirmation and a declaration is this—an affirmation is like complimenting yourself over and over, but a declaration is a more formalized kind of positive statement that is based on a Biblical principle. I had practiced a form of declarations (although I did not know that's what they were called) when I was in law school, but after a while, I fell out of the habit. I suppose I was too busy with my studies, my girlfriends, graduation, working, getting married, getting divorced, getting married again, just dealing with life—pick an excuse. Even during the time when Connie, the boys, and I were super-active in church, I did not take the time to proactively remind myself of God's promises every day.

It is not enough to just read the Bible or say you "believe"—you have to say *what* you want to achieve and then you will start to believe it, and then you will begin to expect things to go in your favor and then you can *apply it to your life*. If God puts a million dollars into my bank account, but I refuse to acknowledge I even have a bank account, the money doesn't do me any good. Each of us is inherently valuable. I realized I needed to start embracing God's promises and *speak them out loud*, again and again.

It is virtually impossible to succeed at something if you do not first believe that you can succeed. Without believing, you have little reason to even try. Negative thinking leads to more negative thinking.

Your thought process is one of the hardest things to control. If you don't agree, try this test: Clear your mind and try to think of nothing for one minute. It is practically impossible. Before you know it, all kinds of random thoughts will begin competing or attention, from needing a drink to needing to go to the bathroom to the fact that you are *trying to think of nothing*. For many, or perhaps most of us, it is easier for thoughts of fear, inferiority, and failure to infect our minds than positive thoughts.

Too many of us allow what we think to control what we speak. But what we speak can also control how we think. If you get control of your words, your thinking will change, and then your life will follow what you believe.

Don't get me wrong—I am not saying that by getting into

the habit of writing and repeating declarations, all your problems will suddenly vanish. They certainly did not for me. However, declarations are the key to improving your attitude about yourself and strengthening your self-confidence, which will enable you to better cope with problems and thereby change your destiny.

,

49

DECLARATIONS

The Holy Spirit inspired me to begin practicing declarations in November of 2003, but I did not know that's what they were called until I heard Joel Osteen talk about them. I had never heard of Joel, but that was about to change. And he was about to change me.

On Thanksgiving Eve in 2005, I drove to Henderson, Kentucky, to see my cousin, Phyllis. She had been a huge help during the last few years of my mother's life. More recently, her husband had committed suicide by shooting himself in front of her. I felt that I should pay her a visit to see how she was doing, having gone through such a traumatic experience.

That night, we were watching television when Joel came on. His message was "Bloom Where You Are Planted." The more I watched, the more I liked him. I had been listening to other television preachers, but Joel was different. For one thing, he was not asking for money. He did not shout; he was just talking in a friendly way, directly to me, it seemed. More importantly, I sensed a vulnerability and humility in him that I had not seen in other televangelists and I was impressed. I started ordering Joel's sermons on CD and DVD. Though it may be common knowledge among his long-time followers, I was surprised to learn he did not want to be a preacher in the beginning of his career, but he had agreed to fill in for his father, a minister, when his father became ill and was hospitalized. He did not believe he was good enough to live up to his father's standards as a preacher. In one of my favorite sermons of Joel's, he describes how he was so nervous his first time behind the pulpit that he had to hold the podium so the audience could not see him shaking.[20] In the sermon, his voice cracks and he becomes visibly emotional as he recalls how the church members believed in him and cheered him on and how, with their support, he became more polished over time. It is a wonderful message about the power of encouragement.

In one of Joel's sermons, he talked about what he called "declarations." As I listened, I realized he was describing the kinds of affirmations I had recently started doing, each from a Biblical foundation. Now, I had a word for them! I wrote four pages of declarations and have written many since then, in various categories such as "Faith," "Confidence," "Strength," and "Wisdom." My first one was based on the Bible verse John 10:10, which reads, *"The thief cometh not, but for to steal, and to kill, and to destroy; I am come that they might have life and that they might have it more abundantly."* My personal declaration, for that one, reads: *"Jesus died not only for my salvation, but also so I can have abundance until it overflows. Jesus is the Good Shepherd and he did gladly lay down his life for me. He loves me that much! A man gets what he believes for in life; nothing more and nothing less."*

I started reading my declarations out loud, first thing in the morning, around noon (unless I was in court or meeting a client), and again before bedtime. Each time took about 15 minutes, which sometimes seemed like an unnecessary distraction, but I forced myself to just do it. *After all,* I thought, *when you have nothing and you are heading downhill toward a cliff, with your hair on fire, what else can you do?* Soon, the declarations became a habit, as easy and as necessary as eating three meals a day. As I repeated them, my thinking began to change. My overall demeanor improved. My stress levels went way down, even though my personal problems kept piling up.

Meanwhile, with the house sold, Connie and I had little time to move into the basement of the office building, which was considerably smaller than the house. Just before Christmas,

---

20   Joel Osteen - Sermon #282: "Bringing Out the Best in People" (DVD)

we moved what furniture would fit into the basement and put the rest in storage. Unable to help carry furniture, I did the only productive thing possible—I went to work. While waiting for the carpet to be installed downstairs, the movers unloaded their truck and spread our furniture along the edge of the rear parking lot. It looked like a yard sale. Passersby stopped and asked if we were throwing the stuff away. Looking out the window at our belongings strewn about the parking lot, I thought, *This is really bad. What has my life become? This sure isn't what Connie expected when she married me.*

A couple of days after settling into our new "home," Connie and I were driving somewhere. Not far away, I noticed a new sign on an office building in the neighborhood, bearing the name of the lawyer who had ripped me off a few years earlier by stealing my clients and my office furnishings. In my mind, I had forgiven him long ago, even though he had not sought forgiveness, but realizing he was now doing business in my neighborhood was like pouring rubbing alcohol into an open wound.

Merry Christmas, I thought. *I sure hope we have a happier New Year.*

50

MIRACLE ON I-30

The first part of 2006 was a little rough, living in a basement. However, Connie and I were gaining such inspiration from Joel Osteen that we decided to splurge on a trip to Houston to see him in person at his world-famous Lakewood Church. To make the most of the trip, we would first take a seven-day, midwinter ocean cruise out of Galveston and later stop in Houston on the way home. Rick had just graduated from college, so we decided to take him and one of his buddies, Pete Birmingham, as a graduation present. I also looked forward to seeing my niece, Lisa, who was a police officer in Houston. We were struggling financially, but after selling the house and consolidating our business loans, we were starting to get back on solid footing. We just needed a breather.

The cruise was just what the doctor ordered. The weather was perfect as we sailed first to Cozumel, then to the Bahamas, and back to Galveston. But the most exciting part, for me, was seeing Joel.

Lakewood Church is one of the biggest in the country, attracting approximately fifty-thousand worshippers every weekend, not to mention millions of television viewers. The church started in an abandoned feed store on the northeast side of Houston but became so popular that it moved to its present location, a former sports arena. After the service, Joel stuck around to greet everyone who wanted to shake his hand. Connie and I patiently waited our turn, along with Rick and Pete.

"Joel, it's really great to meet you," I said as I reached out my hand. "I just want you to know you're really making a difference in my life."

Some people are at first put off by the clenched hand of a quadriplegic, unsure of the proper way to shake it, but Joel gently grasped my curled fingers in his hands and flashed his famous, big-tooth smile.

"God bless you," he said. "Thanks for coming!"

"I know you're busy, Joel, but could I ask you a quick question?"

"Of course."

"I'm a lawyer. I do a lot of bankruptcies and I deal with people who are hurting," I said. "I've been buying your CDs and DVDs. Would you have any objection to me making copies to give to my clients? I won't sell them, and I will make sure everyone understands they are your messages. It would be just to help people."

Joel did not hesitate. "Sure," he said. "My dad always said they belong to God, anyway."

I found Joel to be very humble and kind. He graciously posed for a photo with Rick, Pete, Connie, and me, and we said goodbye. I would later meet him on other occasions, but that first trip to Houston was especially memorable in more ways than one.

As we entered Arkansas, on the way back to Kentucky, Pete offered to take over the driving to give me a break and let me read. The boys unlatched the passenger seat from its base and moved it to the driver's position, then secured my wheelchair to the passenger's side, and off we went.

I had never let anyone else drive my van before. I prefer to be in control whenever possible, but after a while, I got used to Pete being at the wheel and I started to relax and read a book. Heading east on Interstate 30, somewhere southwest of Little Rock, light snow started falling. Soon a thin, white layer covered the pavement. I looked up and realized we were doing about 70 miles per hour in the high-speed lane. There was not as much traffic in that lane, so there were no tire tracks ahead of us like there were in the slow lane, which meant that ours was slicker. A sense of panic jolted me. In hindsight, I believe it was the Holy Spirit warning me to speak up. I almost asked Pete to slow down and move into the center lane, but as soon as the thought crossed my mind, I decided to keep my mouth shut to avoid offending him. I wish I had offended him.

You know those yellow signs that warn "BRIDGE ICES BEFORE ROAD?" Well, they mean what they say. As we drove onto an overpass, the rear of the van began fishtailing from side to side—slightly, at first, and then—WHOOSH! Pete overcompensated by jerking the steering wheel too far, and suddenly we were spinning like an amusement park ride. How many times we did a complete 360, I have no idea, because things were happening so quickly, but when we got to the end of the icy overpass, we hit semi-dry pavement. The sudden traction caused the van to flip sideways. Connie screamed as the van rolled three times. I wasn't consciously counting, but I remember vividly the sound I made each time we went upside-down and the shoulder strap jerked violently against my chest —"Augggh! Augggh! Augggh!" Time seemed to stand still during those few seconds as metal crunched and glass broke. The van stopped flipping but kept sliding on the driver's side for a short distance before hitting an embankment along the right side of the highway, throwing Connie halfway through the driver's side window in the back. She had been lying down in the backseat, with her seatbelt unbuckled and Rick next to her, on the floor. Connie ordinarily wore a seatbelt, but there was no comfortable way for her to lie down without unbuckling it. Now, she was wedged between the ground and the minivan. If the vehicle had not stopped at the exact spot where it did, on a slight depression in the ground, she surely would have been cut in half. Luckily, she was conscious.

"Is everyone okay?" Rick yelled. "Mom, are you okay?"

"I think so," she mumbled. "Ron? Where's Ron?"

"I'm all right," I gasped, "but it's hard to breathe. The seat belt's cuttin' into my chest."

Rick twisted his way between my chair and the driver's seat, holding me up to relieve the pressure from the shoulder harness.

His head was bleeding from shards of glass embedded in his skin. My head was jammed up against the ceiling, which was mashed in. Although I was still strapped into my wheelchair, my left leg had fallen from its previous position under the dashboard and my foot was on the steering wheel. As I tried to adjust to a more tolerable position, my foot kicked the CD player, causing it to turn on. Joel Osteen's voice came blaring through the speakers: *"Are you discouraged today because you're facing a difficult battle? We all have things that come against us in life..."*

"Turn that off!" Rick yelled.

I am sure he meant no disrespect to Joel, but under the circumstances, he was in no mood for a sermon.

By now, other motorists were starting to pull over. Someone outside the van yelled, "Look out!" as a car skidded past us, barely missing our van. From my position inside the van, I couldn't see what was happening outside, but the thought of a potential impact and the "whooshing" sound of the out-of-control car terrified me for two or three seconds until it stopped.

I was shivering. I had often been outside without a coat during the winter, pushing my wheelchair a short distance. However, I had never realized how cold thirty-two degrees could be until that moment, trapped in the wreckage of an overturned minivan. First responders arrived within a few minutes and used the "Jaws of Life" to cut us out. They rushed us to a hospital in Little Rock, where doctors determined Connie was not hurt seriously (a diagnosis which later turned out to be incorrect). Doctors picked small pieces of glass from Rick's forehead. Pete did not seem to be hurt. As far as my condition was concerned, the ER staff, for some reason, did not think it necessary to check me for a possible head injury. (I discovered later that I had probably suffered a concussion.)

After a few hours in the ER, the hospital released us. There we were, injured and stranded in Little Rock, without transportation, still reeling from the shock of the accident. Before we left the hospital, a Good Samaritan-type of woman generously offered to help us. She was a great, wonderful "God" person—an example of the kind who quietly helps people without fanfare or recognition. She had a ministry that helped people who wound up at the hospital and needed food, money, or emergency shelter. She drove us to a nearby hotel and got us a room—one for all four of us. I wish I had gotten her name and contact information because I did not properly thank her, but in our state of shock at that time, none of us thought to take notes.

Rick and Pete felt good enough to get away from the hotel every now and then, but Connie and I stayed in bed for the next 30 hours, sleeping most of the time, but occasionally waking to take muscle relaxers. Every time I tried to move, my neck would spasm like a painful charley horse. Connie was also experiencing pains in her chest.

On the second day following the accident, Connie's dad, who by then lived six hours away in McMinnville, Tennessee, came to pick us up. While he was driving us to Kentucky, the hospital called to inform us that the doctors had misread Connie's X-rays and that her sternum was "crushed and shattered." *Well, that would explain her pain!* I thought. I hardly spoke all the way home. I realized later my uncharacteristic silence for such a long time was probably an indication I had suffered a concussion. Doctors also later diagnosed me with a nerve impingement (yes, another one) in my neck as a result of the wreck. I still have it to this day, and though it does not cause me any great difficulty, it hurts to turn my head sideways. Clearly, the hospital should not have released us so soon after the accident. If the same thing had happened to one of my clients, I might have recommended hiring a medical malpractice lawyer. However, I have never been litigious when it comes to my own misfortunes.

As terrible as the accident was and the inferior medical attention that we received, I am convinced our survival was nothing short of a miracle. You might wonder why God did not simply keep us from having the accident in the first place. Wouldn't that have been a more impressive miracle? I have thought about that many times. Maybe it was God's way of teaching Pete he should drive more carefully. Maybe it was his way of teaching me I should pay closer attention when the Holy Spirit tells me to speak up. All I know for certain is that four people survived a wreck that probably should have killed them. For that, I am extremely grateful.

51

SPLISH SPLASH

It took three weeks after the accident in Arkansas to settle the insurance claim and get money to buy another minivan and another four weeks to have a wheelchair-accessible model delivered. Connie spent most of her time during that period recuperating at home since not much can be done for a crushed sternum besides resting and taking pain medications.

The advantage of living in the basement under my office was that it made getting to work without a vehicle a whole lot easier. The disadvantage was—well, it was a basement.

Now that we had transportation again, we looked forward to going back to church. Early one Sunday morning in March, the alarm went off, as usual. Mentally, I hit the snooze button with the intention of catching a few extra Z's while Connie made coffee. As she sat up and swung her legs over the side of the bed, my sleep was suddenly disturbed by two unfamiliar sounds—a gentle splash followed by an expletive which I had rarely heard Connie use.

"What's wrong?" I asked.

"There's water on the floor!" she said. "The basement's flooded!"

"How much?" I asked.

"It looks like about three inches."

"Oh, crap," I said.

It had been raining heavily that weekend, and the storm sewer had backed up into the basement. At least, it wasn't the sanitary sewer, but any kind of flood is bad. Was this our new normal? I mean, were we now supposed to expect a disaster every month? We had filed for bankruptcy in November, moved into a basement in December, survived a car wreck in February, and now a flood in March.

At that moment, I was not too thrilled with my life. Don't get me wrong; I did not blame God for the present situation any more than I blamed him for any of the other horrible things that had happened in my life. Matthew 5:45 says *He maketh His sun to rise on the evil and on the good, and sendeth rain on the just and on the unjust.* I just wished that God would sendeth a little less rain.

I figured it was time for my daily declarations. If I was serious about them, I could not do them just when I felt good. So, with Connie sloshing around the basement, I lay in bed and reminded myself, *out loud*, how God's promises apply to my life:

"I am happy, positive and victorious!" (*"A righteous man may have many troubles, but the Lord delivers him from them all."* – *Psalm 34:19*)

"I trust that God has a special plan for my life!" (*"And we know that in all things, God works for the good of those who love Him, who have been called according to His purpose."* – *Romans 8:28*)

"I will cherish every moment that makes me smile!" (*"God is able to do far more abundantly beyond all that we ask or think, according to the power that works within us."* – *Ephesions 3:20*).

Connie and I skipped church that morning. Our shoes were wet and we needed to start drying out the basement and salvage whatever we could. We managed to reach some friends, who helped us rent a water pump and get it situated. Since the basement was at ground level in the rear of the building, we ran the hose out the backdoor and pumped the water into the parking lot, which sloped downhill toward a drain. It took several hours to get the water out and then a few days to dry everything with fans. By the end of the week, the basement was pretty much back to normal, which meant that it was dreary, dark and cold, but livable. For now, it was home.

52

THE JOEL EFFECT

I was not marking the calendar, but roughly forty days and forty nights after our little flood, the clouds parted and the sun came out for Connie and me, just like in the story of Noah. There may have even been a rainbow. It sure felt like it!

In early spring, a couple of friends who knew of our plight offered to let Connie and me move into a little house they owned in the town of Ludlow, just a few miles away, across the Ohio River from Cincinnati. To help us get back on our feet, they agreed to let us live rent-free for up to one year, with the understanding we would pay a modest fee thereafter. As it turned out, I was able to start paying rent after six months. Our friends did not ask for early payment, but I would not have felt right taking advantage of them for six more months without paying.

The business started picking up, which I attributed, in large part, to the declarations I had been dutifully reciting each day. I believed they were instrumental in helping me to change my outlook by bringing not just my expectations, but my *actions* in line with my spiritual beliefs. The words I uttered affected my overall demeanor, which had an impact on the people in my life—friends, clients, colleagues, and judges. People are naturally drawn to others who exude confidence. Whether it was obvious to others or just to myself, God was at the center of everything I did, directly or indirectly, from morning till night. Things seemed to start going my way, and within three years, I was able to give more money to charity than I had ever earned in a year.

I did not lose sight of the fact my good financial fortune depended on other people's negative situations. However, the same could be said of firefighters, police officers, doctors, and plumbers. I was not exploiting people's misfortunes; I was trying to help make their lives better; showing them that not only could I fix their legal problems, but I actually cared about them.

Increasingly, I was getting more opportunities to share with my clients what God had done for me and what he could do for them. Every day, I dealt with many people who were at the lowest point of their life—often broke, sometimes addicted, occasionally suicidal. Whenever someone expressed an interest, I eagerly talked about God. There was even a prayer box in the lobby, with a form that visitors could fill out anonymously and drop in if they wished. Prayer requests were disseminated to Lakewood Church and other churches, meaning that each need was prayed for by thousands of believers. I was going from being an attorney who was a Christian to being a Christian attorney. Sometimes I spent more time discussing clients' personal problems than their legal issues. And there was no better conversation starter for God than one very special photo.

After returning home from that first trip to Houston, I placed a framed photo of Joel Osteen, Connie, Rick, Pete, and me on my desk. Oftentimes, clients and other visitors would notice the picture and say something like, "Hey, isn't that preacher on TV?" Some knew his name, some did not, but invariably the photo would open the door to a conversation about God. In the months and years that followed, Connie and I went to see Joel speak in other cities—sometimes just the two of us and other times with church groups. But in 2006, within months of that first encounter, Joel was already blessing me and inspiring many of my clients in ways he could not possibly have known.

Remember, Joel had given me permission to make copies of his sermons and distribute them to clients, free of charge, so that's what I did. No matter what kind of personal problem somebody would share with me, I could open my file cabinet and find a relevant message, which I would give to that person.

I started sending sermons to everyone on my mailing list who requested them.

I do not know how many sermons Joel Osteen has delivered through the years, but I believe there are about five basic messages from all his teachings, at least one of which applies directly to every client who has ever walked into my office. In almost every case, my clients' problems have stemmed, in one way or another, from thinking negatively about themselves or from poor expectations, which leads to similar thoughts about other people. Jesus said, "Love your neighbor as you love yourself," but unfortunately, many people don't like themselves very much, which influences how they relate to others. I found Joel's sermons to be so impactful that I took time to transcribe some of them, word for word, so I could break them down, study them, and understand how to apply them to different situations.

When you sit around talking negatively, you begin to think negatively. There is nothing new about that concept; I began to understand it shortly after I became paralyzed, and later, from the teachings of Dale Carnegie, Zig Ziglar, and others. But Joel Osteen took positive thinking and combined it with the scriptural support to give a literal view of what God has promised us all. Joel took the concept of declarations to a new level by making them more personal.

The photo that Ron keeps on his desk. Though it was taken in 2006, it was autographed in 2007. Left to right: Pete Birmingham, Joel Osteen, Connie Adams, Ron Adams and Rick Adams.

53

WRONG NUMBER, RIGHT CALL

Some people say a miracle is an amazing event that happens supernaturally. *Mirriam-Webster.com* defines "miracle" as "an extraordinary event taken as a sign of the power of God." That is what happened to my law practice. Skeptics will scoff, but I know in my heart that what occurred was guided by the hand of a higher power.

In 2007, I had one full-time and one part-time legal assistant. There was more demand for my services than I could handle and I was turning clients away. I needed help quickly.

Out of the blue, I received a call from an old friend who had moved away four years earlier. He and his wife had met Connie and me in the Sunday School class we used to teach. A friend of his, who was managing one of the biggest law firms in Kentucky, had recently moved to my area and was commuting one-hundred-twenty miles to work every day. He asked if I knew of any openings at a law firm close to where she was living now. I told him to send me his friend's resume. Her name was Bernice.

Bernice Zeller was used to running a law office of sixty staff members. She was way over-qualified for my modest practice, and I ordinarily would not have wasted time calling her, but I decided to take a chance since my friend had spoken so highly of her. Also, because Bernice and her husband were in my friend's Sunday School class, I knew she was a Christian. That was not a requirement for the job, but I considered it an attribute. After we prayed over the phone and thought about the situation, we decided to meet two weeks later.

"Please call me Bernie," she said.

Having worked for a major law firm, Bernie was used to making more money than I was making at that time. There was no way I could afford her, but we both felt strongly that God had brought us together. Bernie liked me, I liked her, and my office was close to where she was living. I promised that as soon as God blessed my law firm, I would give her incremental raises until she got back to what she was used to making and more. We both made concessions and she accepted the job as my vice president of operations.

I took a personal pay cut to twelve dollars an hour so I could afford to pay Bernie two-thirds of what she made at her previous job. To some people, that might seem unfair since I owned the practice, but it was necessary at the time to get the office back on firm footing. The strategy worked.

As soon as Bernie was onboard, business took off. Thanks in large part to her amazing management skills, we went from handling an average of three cases per month to twenty. Soon, I hired Ruth Reyer, an independent marketing consultant, to help with business development.

"Ruth, we need to hire someone to answer the phone," Bernie said. "You and I have too many other things to do."

Ruth made a few calls and almost immediately found Pam, who was coming out of a negative personal situation and needed a job. She had no experience working in a law office, but when I interviewed her, I was so impressed with her positive attitude and desire to learn and work hard that I hired her on the spot.

I had been competitive my whole life, but after adding three top-notch staffers; I was now concerned my practice was growing too fast. Revenues were up and all the bills were being paid, but as the only attorney in the firm, I could only handle so much. I decided to slow down the pace, but God had other plans. One day I dialed the phone with the intention of calling Ruth to discuss some business, but someone else answered.

"Hello?" she said.

"May I speak to Ruth, please?" I asked.

"Who?"

"Ruth Reyer."

"I'm sorry, but you have the wrong number," the voice said.

"Wait a minute," I said. "You sound familiar. Do I know you? My name is Ron Adams."

"Ron!" she nearly shouted. "This is Elena! How have you been?"

Elena had worked for me a few years earlier but had since got married and moved away.

"I'm a little confused," I admitted. "Were you just now calling me? I was trying to reach one of my associates, but when I dialed the phone, you answered."

"No, I wasn't calling you," she said. "You called me."

I thought for a moment, trying to wrap my mind around what had just happened.

"But I don't even know your number," I said.

"Isn't it programmed into your phone?"

"No, I didn't have this phone system when you worked here," I said. "I have no idea how I called you."

"Maybe you just remembered my number."

"I don't think you ever gave me your new number after you moved away," I said. "Besides, I have a good memory, but not that good."

"Huh!" she said. "Well, it's great to hear from you, anyway."

"Hey, Elena, I know this may be a long shot, but by any chance are you looking for a job?"

"You mean with you? Are you kidding?" she said. "I was just praying with my mom for a job in a Christian work environment!"

Elena started working for me again, two days later. How could I not hire her after God had guided my hand to dial a "wrong" number that turned out to be just what I needed! It was no mere coincidence.

I have experienced many miracles, but never so many in so short a period as in 2007. You might say, "What's so special about what happened that year?" Here is how I would answer: Not all miracles are like the parting of the Red Sea or Jesus bringing

221

Lazarus back from the dead. Some are like little pawns on a chess board, seemingly insignificant, but playing an important role in God's long-term plan. In 2007, four extraordinary people came into my life, unexpectedly, at just the time I desperately needed help running and growing my law practice. To me, they were miracles.

54

His Well

Vincent Van Gogh once said, "Great things are done by a series of small things brought together." Sometimes it truly is the seemingly insignificant gestures that make a big difference, like a bolt that helps hold a bridge together. Any of us can brighten someone's day with a smile, a kind word, a phone call. Or maybe a little flower vase, bought with pop bottle money, given by a young boy to his mother.

By 2007, business had picked back up to the point where I could afford to help other people financially, within reason. For obvious reasons, I have always had a special place in my heart for disabled people, as well as first responders, so I established two scholarship funds—one for children of first responders and the other, which I named the Lady Ruth Adams Scholarship, in memory of my mother—to help disabled students pay for college. Separate from the scholarships, I also began donating about $25 or $50 from each bankruptcy case to a children's hospital, letting each client know that I was doing it, not for any self-aggrandizement, but to demonstrate how great it feels to give back.

It was very gratifying to help others financially, but I also was driven to help them spiritually. Eventually, I realized I was doing almost as much ministry work as legal work out of my office. For several reasons—financial, tax, and ethical—I needed to separate the spiritual from the legal. Ethics rules require lawyers to keep their business separate from anything else, so I set up the ministry as a 501(c)(3) nonprofit organization. After discussing ideas with my office staff, I decided to call the ministry His Well.

A well is where people go to get filled; it is a source of replenishment. Jesus is the source of eternal life. As the Bible says, his "well" is the one that never runs dry! If we claim to be followers of Christ, we need to emulate him to the best of our ability and do what he says is important. When someone repeats something three times, you know they mean business. In the New Testament (John 21:15-17) Jesus does exactly that when he asks Peter, three times, "Do you love me?" Peter responds, "Lord, you know I love you," and each time, Jesus tells him to "Feed my sheep." The specific words vary, depending on which translation of the Bible you are reading, but the meaning is clear—Jesus wants his followers to feed others—not necessarily with just food, but with spiritual nourishment and love.

Good things begin with a conversation and there is no better conversation starter than doing something nice for someone. His Well consisted of volunteers performing random acts of kindness for a lot of people—many of them strangers. Our motto was: *Share for no reason other than to share. Serve for no reason other than to serve. Love for no reason other than to love.* Each volunteer was equipped with a "blessing bag" full of simple items like gloves, caps, scarves, lotion, lip balm, sunscreen, bottled water, and such, which were handed out to people as needed. There were no strings attached or requirements to listen to a religious message, but if someone wanted to know more about the purpose behind His Well, our volunteers were prepared and eager to talk about God. If desired, they would give the person a copy of declarations that had helped me get through hard times (and still do). You will find them at the end of this book.

Another part of His Well, which proved to be particularly popular in some of our local communities, was a program called "Baked to Bless." Volunteers baked cookies and distributed them twice a week to fire houses, police departments, and nursing homes. Not everyone wanted to discuss Jesus, but I don't think anyone ever turned away our tasty treats.

Perhaps the most important aspect of His Well was our prayer chain, a multistate network of "prayer warriors" who took turns praying for anyone who needed a miracle in their life. Anyone can pray, at any time, even alone. But when you have a group of believers praying for the same person, it creates a bond among those involved, allowing them to connect with each other and with God in a more powerful way. It's sort of like the difference between watching a basketball game on television by yourself at home and cheering for your favorite team in a packed arena with thousands of like-minded fans. It may be psychological, but a crowd generates more energy, and those who are being cheered, or prayed for, can feel it.

There was a "prayer box" in my office, in which visitors could drop notes requesting prayers for themselves or others. Most prayer requests involved health-related issues. The second most common category of requests involved prayers for someone's children, a spouse, or a friend to overcome an addiction or to become a better person in some way. The third most common type of request was financial. Not surprisingly, many financial prayer requests were associated with health issues because health problems often prevent people from working and can result in high medical bills.

Many of our prayer warriors volunteered to take prayer requests during specific blocks of time, which resulted in believers praying in shifts for those in need, 24/7. I cannot tell you how many times we heard back from people who shared with us how God had answered a specific prayer. Matthew 21:22 says, *If you believe, you will receive whatever you ask for in prayer.* That does not mean God will literally grant any request, or that he will do so as quickly as we want. But I believe there is power in prayer, and I know for a fact our prayer chain worked.

All the "little things" our volunteers were doing—the blessing bags, the declarations, the homemade cookies, the prayers— were making an impact. So were the sermons that Joel Osteen had given me permission to distribute on CD years earlier, which were now in such demand that I purchased a professional CD burner capable of making several copies at a time. By the end of

2008, His Well had mailed out approximately twenty-thousand copies of Joel's sermons on CD, at no charge. Joel was not involved with His Well, but his influence was palpable.

His Well was first and foremost a ministry, but it was also a way of connecting members socially. Oftentimes, volunteers would get together for fun or to attend a special event. Once, when Joel was coming to Cincinnati for one of his "A Night of Hope" services, I arranged for about fifty of our members to volunteer. We all rode together on a chartered bus owned by one of our people. Members of our group were scattered throughout the arena, performing their respective tasks. It took me longer to exit the arena, partly because of where I had been working but also because there were many people in wheelchairs, and each elevator could only accommodate six at a time.

I was both thrilled and disappointed to learn that Joel and his wife, Victoria, had come aboard the bus to greet everyone, and I had missed them by just a few minutes. It reminded me of the time the band Journey stopped at my T-shirt shop while I was away at law school and I missed the opportunity to meet them. Still, it gave me a good feeling to think about how His Well was serving so many people in so many ways and to recognize Joel's inspiration.

I was so grateful to Joel that when he returned to Cincinnati for another "A Night of Hope" in 2016, His Well sponsored a prayer breakfast with him. About 20 local pastors and Christian business leaders were invited to attend the breakfast at a hotel. Connie and I went with Ruth Reyer, the business development director for my law office, who was instrumental in organizing our part of the event. Seeing Joel speak on television or on stage in front of a crowd is inspiring enough but spending time with him in an informal setting is all the more uplifting. He is the same behind the scenes as he is on camera—warm, humble, encouraging. During the breakfast, Joel sat at the head table while his mother, Dodie Osteen, sat with Connie, Ruth, and me a bit farther back. We chatted about our families; she talked about how shy Joel used to be as a young man and how she and her late husband, John, had made a habit of leading Joel and his five siblings in prayer every morning before they went to school. It was wonderful getting to know Dodie, the matriarch of the Osteen family and former co-pastor of the original Lakewood Church with her husband, which has since grown into an international spiritual powerhouse under Joel's leadership. I will always remember Dodie's kindness at that prayer breakfast.

His Well was never intended to emulate Joel Osteen Ministries or any of the other big charitable organizations that have multimillion-dollar budgets and thousands of employees which feed the hungry and provide medical and disaster relief services and such. Those are wonderful and necessary, but I started His Well to serve individuals on a smaller, more intimate scale. Though the organization was separate from my legal practice, it allowed me the ability to connect with clients and other people who were hurting, to help them in ways that were so much more meaningful than just addressing their immediate legal problems. I was not running a church, but in some ways, His Well functioned as one.

Ron and Connie Adams with Dodie Osteen, Joel Osteen's mother, at a prayer breakfast in Cincinnati in 2016. (Photo by Ruth Reyer)

55

Back to Life

Financially, the next few years were better than ever as the law practice thrived, but I had been through so many ups and downs before that I never took anything for granted. Unfortunately, life was about to take another turn for the worse.

I was having some dental work done, which was expected to take several hours. When the dentist left me alone to tend to another patient, I dozed off in the office recliner, with my hands resting in my lap. As I slept, my arms fell to my sides and I was jolted awake by a sudden, sharp pain in my left shoulder. I would soon learn that the jerking of my arm had torn my rotator cuff.

The pain subsided after a few days but never went away completely and periodically would throb uncontrollably. My range of motion became even more limited than before, which meant I could no longer do most things I had learned to do by myself, like getting in and out of the wheelchair, taking showers, and driving a van. After a few months of enduring the pain and the many inconveniences it caused, I decided to have an operation to fix my shoulder.

An anesthesiologist did a nerve block to numb my shoulder. The outpatient procedure went according to plan, but the doctor cautioned me that I would have a lot of pain during recovery at home. He wrote me a prescription for Percocet®, a powerful medication, which he advised me to take every six hours to stay ahead of the pain. Any opioid can impair one's mind, but as a quadriplegic whose nervous system was already compromised, I also had to worry about how it might affect my breathing. Despite my trepidation about the drug, my shoulder was hurting badly, so I took a pill and went to bed as the doctor ordered. I have no memory of what happened next, so I will describe it as it was told to me…

It stormed that night. I tossed and turned next to Connie, somehow ending up with my head on her chest. The skylight above the bed revealed flashes of lightning. A loud clap of thunder jolted Connie awake. As another lightning bolt illuminated the room for a split second, she saw that my face was blue. I had gone into respiratory failure. She shook me.

"Ron! Ron!"

Connie dialed 911 and began to perform CPR, remembering what our son Rick, who was by then a registered nurse, had once told her: *If anything happens to Dad, forget everything you have ever heard about CPR, and just beat the hell out of his chest.*[21]

So that is what she did. With every ounce of strength, fueled by adrenaline, powered by fear and anger and desperation, she pounded my chest with her clenched hands. I was unresponsive. She kept going. By the time the paramedics arrived, I was dead.

They rushed me to St. Elizabeth West Hospital on the off chance I could be revived. When I regained consciousness, I had no idea where I was or what had just occurred. I still felt woozy from the pain medication I had taken hours before, not to mention whatever other drugs the paramedics and hospital staff had injected into my body.

The next day (or was it two days later?), my nieces, Kathy and Lisa, came to the hospital. Kathy, who is Lolo's daughter, drove down from Ohio. Lisa, who is Joyce's daughter, flew in from Houston. It reminded me of the time I woke up in the hospital after my coal mining accident and thought I was dying because family members had come hundreds of miles to see me. Only this time, I did not think I was dying. I was alive, thanks to the paramedics, doctors, and nurses who did not give up on me, but

---

21   This should not be construed as medical advice. CPR can cause serious injuries if not performed properly. When possible, it should be performed by someone who has been trained and certified.

mostly because of Connie, who is convinced my survival was nothing short of a miracle from God.

"I think Ron was dead on top of me," she told someone. "That lightning and thunder woke me at just the right time to see him and know what to do."

56

THE PANAMA CONNECTION

Few issues have divided America more than abortion. Imagine how conflicted I felt after learning that I might be cured one day, but only if an innocent baby died.

The first time I heard about stem cell research was in 2001 when President George W. Bush signed an executive order restricting the use of federal funds for that purpose. Stem cells are types of cells that can transform into various other types of cells and become organs. Scientists had been studying them since the 1960s, but it was not until the late 1980s that a method was discovered to clone stem cells from human embryos, paving the way for the possibility of restoring or replacing defective organs. There was, and still is, optimism in the scientific community for the potential of stem cells to cure many diseases and treat disabilities, including spinal cord injuries. However, this kind of research has been controversial, particularly among many Christians and others who oppose abortion.

Having been paralyzed for my entire adult life, I was naturally intrigued by the prospect of a medical procedure that might cure me. How many times had I asked God for such a miracle? What I wouldn't give to play basketball, walk down the street, open a door by myself and not have to struggle to get through it—to do all the things that others take for granted but which, for me, are a never-ending source of frustration! I was willing to try anything. Except *that*.

Being against abortion, all I could think of was the propaganda I had been hearing about how stem cell research involved aborted fetuses and how poor women would be motivated to get pregnant and have abortions just to make money from their unborn babies. Now, I know better.

I hate to say this, but sometimes well-meaning Christians and politicians inadvertently spread misinformation in the name of Jesus before they understand all the facts. In reality, not all stem cells used in scientific research come from aborted fetuses. Much stem cell research involves cells harvested from the placenta and/or the umbilical cord, which is disposed of, anyway, after a baby is born. It boggles my mind to think of the googolplexes[22] of potentially useful cells that have been wasted because the U.S. government does not distinguish between a living fetus and an otherwise useless umbilical cord when it comes to funding research. It's like throwing the baby out with the bathwater (no pun intended).

While stem cell research has stagnated in the U.S., it has been moving forward in other countries, where, in some cases, scientists have reported promising results. Though it is greatly restricted, a few medical facilities in America offer stem cell therapy on a limited basis, mostly under the radar. I learned of one such place and, after checking it out, decided to try it in 2018.

In the long term, I was interested in the possibility that stem cell therapy might one day cure me of my paralysis. However, my short-term goal was to reduce the pain in my left shoulder, which had never completely gone away following the incident in the dentist's office. I also was hoping to speed the healing of a large bedsore that had developed as a result of my prolonged recovery in bed following my near-death experience. (With quadriplegia, one medical issue can often lead to another, including bedsores.) Connie, meanwhile, was going to receive stem cell therapy for pain from a herniated disc, which had been bothering her for years.

My professional caregiver traveled with Connie and me to New England. We got up at 4:30 a.m. and flew out of the Greater

---

22   A googolplex is a 1 followed by 100 zeroes; the largest number named with a single word.

Cincinnati-Northern Kentucky International Airport at 7:00, arriving in Boston two hours later. We then rode in a wheelchair-accessible cab to a medical facility, which I will not name because I am not sure of the legality of the procedure and I do not want to get the clinic in trouble.

The procedure was simple—Connie and I each received two injections into our arms. I also received one injection in each of my shoulders and Connie received four injections in her lower back. The procedure took three hours, and then we rode back to the airport and arrived home in Kentucky by 8:30 p.m., which made for an exhausting sixteen-hour day.

The stem cell treatment in New England was not cheap. The bill came to about thirty thousand dollars, which of course, was not covered by medical insurance, but it was worth it. Within a couple of days, my shoulder felt better than it had in a long time and I regained a level of mobility that enabled me to resume driving. My chronic bedsore also began to heal so quickly that my personal physician called me a "healing machine." Connie also felt better. I cannot prove that a single stem cell therapy session was the reason for our sudden improvement. Some doctors might argue that Connie's and my respective recoveries were psychosomatic. But I was now feeling so optimistic about this kind of therapy that I decided to take it a step further.

I had heard about a place called the Stem Cell Institute in Panama City, Panama, which was offering experimental stem cell treatments for certain types of spinal cord injuries, mine included. I am well aware of medical quacks and scam artists who sell "snake oil" to gullible people, so I was not about to jump into something that sounded too good to be true. I was determined to research, to the best of my ability, the science behind the treatment in question and the clinic that was offering it. I read all the articles I could find, watched videos, and listened to many tapes on the subject.

One of the first things I learned, which made me feel comfortable with the Stem Cell Institute, is they are very selective when accepting candidates for their studies. They are not looking to make money from desperate people if the doctors do not believe there is a good chance of success. Also, the stem cells used to treat spinal cord injuries are harvested from umbilical cords, not from human fetuses.

Since my spinal cord injury had occurred more than ten years prior, the clinic initially rejected me for the first study that I inquired about because it was less likely to be successful, considering my age. I wrote back and asked if there were other protocols for which I might be considered. As it turned out, the clinic was conducting a study called a Longevity and Frailty Protocol, which the doctor said might be helpful in my case because it involved using the same types of cells that were being used in the spinal cord study. Of course, he could make no promises. I decided to take a chance.

I did not discuss my interest in stem cell therapy with doctors with whom I had been dealing because most doctors in the U.S. tend to be very conservative. Even though stem cell therapy is generally accepted as a legitimate field of research, it is not widely taught in U.S. medical schools, so most American doctors do not understand it, and, therefore, they are reluctant to discuss it or recommend such treatments. There was, however, one exception. I had to tell my family doctor about my plan in order to get his medical approval to fly to Panama.

"Well, Ron, you know I can't recommend this kind of treatment because it's not proven, and it's not legal in the U.S.," he said.

"I understand that," I said. "I've been reading a lot about stem cell therapy and I've researched the clinic in Panama. It seems to have a good reputation."

"You're right about that," the doctor conceded. "Even though there doesn't appear to be any evidence the treatment can actually re-grow your nerve cells, there don't seem to be any negative side effects. If you really want to try it, I won't stop you."

Connie and I arrived in Panama City and taxied straight to the Panama Hilton. The Stem Cell Institute was located on the 63rd floor of an adjacent skyscraper, which was connected to the hotel.

The next morning, before my appointment, we were on our way to an outside terrace, after eating breakfast in the hotel restaurant, when—CLUNK, CLUNK, CRASH!—my wheelchair suddenly bounced down two steps and I toppled over sideways, landing hard on the marble floor in the lobby. Connie tried to catch me but lost her footing and ended up lying next to me, moaning in pain. We were quickly surrounded by hotel employees, snapping pictures as if I were a movie star and they were the paparazzi. I remained strapped in my chair, sideways, for twenty minutes, looking like a *Cirque du Soleil* acrobat frozen in mid-air, waiting for the hotel paramedic to arrive and determine if it was safe for me to be moved to an upright position. Part of one of the wheel covers had broken off and one of my leg braces was slightly bent, but other than that, I was okay and my chair was still functional. Connie, on the other hand, was badly bruised and in pain, but not seriously hurt.

Judging by the hotel staff's prompt reaction with multiple cameras, I guessed I was not the first person to take a tumble on those steps. What had happened was that the color of the upper floor, where the restaurant was situated, blended with that of the floor below, making the steps practically invisible. Why they were not marked with caution tape, or why there were no handrails or a wheelchair ramp, was inexplicable. Even if such safety measures were not legally required in Panama, you would think that a major hotel would install them anyway to prevent mishaps!

My doctor at the Stem Cell Center was notified of the accident and came down to the lobby to examine me. Fortunately, I was able to proceed with the stem cell treatment for which I had flown 2,100 miles and already paid thousands of dollars.

The procedure was simple and painless. Each day, for three days, an IV tube was inserted into each arm for ten minutes to allow millions of stem cells to flow into my bloodstream. Then, I received four injections of stem cells into my shoulders. Aft each treatment, Connie and I did some sightseeing and ther after the third treatment, we flew home.

Did it work? Not yet, but I was not expecting immediate results. From the get-go, I was under no delusion that stem cell therapy would be a quick fix to my life-long disability. The procedure is still experimental, and although there have been some promising results, I was told it can take multiple treatments over months, or even years, for the cells to communicate with each other in their mysterious way and figure out what kind of tissue they need to become. I am still waiting, but obviously, I remain hopeful.

57

NOT THE END

There was not one magical moment when I became a Christian. I did not have an epiphany or a "Road to Damascus" conversion, as happened to Saul in the New Testament.[23] For me, acceptance of Jesus was more an evolutionary process than a sudden realization.

Though I was born into a "Christian" family, my early understanding of what it meant to be a Christ follower was incomplete and flawed. You cannot simply be born a Christian any more than you are born a Democrat or a Republican. Becoming one is a conscious choice, not something you inherit from your parents. (By the way, no political party has exclusivity with God.)

People believe in God, or choose not to believe for different reasons. The same is true when it comes to Jesus. Was he merely a prophet, a philosopher, a teacher, or something else? I believe that he was, and is, the Son of God—the Messiah. Although I knew about Jesus and believed in him at an early age, it was not until years later, as a lawyer, that I began to analyze my beliefs in terms of the evidence.

The existence of God and the deity of Jesus cannot be proven in the way I would prove a legal case or a scientist would prove something in a laboratory. My faith is based on a combination of facts, feelings, and personal experiences. Theologians, historians,

---

23   Acts 9:3-19

and others who are smarter than I have written entire books on the subject, but a few general points I think make the most sense include:

- Archaeologists have found evidence that corroborates many aspects of the New Testament, while nothing in the New Testament has been disproved.
- The first-century Jewish historian Flavius Josephus and the ancient Roman historian Tacitus each wrote about Jesus as a real person who lived and was executed in Judea.[24]
- Many early followers of Christ chose to be persecuted and even executed rather than renounce their belief in him. They were living in a time when eyewitnesses to Jesus were still alive. They were convinced of his divinity for a reason.
- In spite of its human flaws and mistakes, Christianity has survived for 2,000 years. If Jesus were a crazy man or a con artist, the movement he started likely would have died off centuries ago.
- As authors Josh McDowell (a former agnostic) and Sean McDowell, Ph.D., point out, "The Bible, compared with other ancient writings, has more manuscript evidence than any ten pieces of classical literature combined."[25]
- Jesus fulfilled several hundred Old Testament prophecies that foreshadowed the coming of the Messiah.

My purpose is not to force my beliefs on anyone, but if you are curious about Jesus, I suggest starting by taking some quality time and reading the four Gospels, each of which describes Jesus' life from the perspective of its respective author, who either knew him personally or knew those who were close to him. Matthew, a tax collector, and John, a fisherman, were among the Twelve Apostles. Mark was a follower of the Apostle Peter and was an evangelist. Luke, a physician, was a friend of Paul of Tarsus. I

---

24 https://www.history.com/news/was-jesus-real-historical-evidence
25 Josh McDowell and Sean McDowell, Evidence That Demands a Verdict: Life-Changing Truth for a Skeptical World (Nashville: Thomas Nelson, 2017 [revised edition])

know there is debate among scholars as to the actual authorship of the Gospels, but I believe they were written under the guidance of the Holy Spirit. As you read about how Jesus taught, loved, and cared for people, he is just so wonderful. When I was younger, I did not know all the great things he did and the insightful things he said, but Jesus was with me, even before I knew his name. He is equally available to everyone.

From the beginning of civilization, people have looked up at the night sky and wondered, "How did it all begin?"

The late astronomer Carl Sagan was famous for pointing out that "billions and billions" of stars exist in the universe, each of which is a sun. Of all the planets revolving around all those suns, ours is the only one that is known to harbor life. Many people mistakenly believe that Sagan was an atheist when, in fact, he was a self-avowed agnostic. He was once quoted in *The Washington Post* as saying, "An atheist has to know a lot more than I know. An atheist is someone who knows there is no God."[26] Likewise, Albert Einstein had as much disdain for atheists as he did for religious zealots. Though he did not believe in a personal god, organized religion or an afterlife, he alluded many times to the possibility of a higher power in the universe, once calling it "too vast for our limited minds" to comprehend.[27]

Many people dismiss the existence of God by criticizing him for allowing bad things to happen. As I am finishing this memoir, I have just learned that my personal assistant, Lisa, with whom Connie and I had become very close, was killed in a car wreck. She lived in an apartment in the basement of our home, and each day she would help me get ready for work and run errands. On the day she died, we went through our usual routine. She cheerfully wished me a "Happy Friday" and walked out the door. A few hours later, I was devastated to learn that she was a passenger in a car that ran into the back of a truck. Her son, who was driving, was not injured. Connie and I are distraught, but just as everyone must deal with things that don't make sense, we will get through it.

---

26 Joel Achenbach, "Carl Sagan denied being an atheist. So what did he believe? [Part 1]," *The Washington Post,* July 10, 2014.

27 Viereck, George Sylvester (1930). *Glimpses of the Great.* New York: The Macaulay Company, pp. 372-373.

I do not understand why innocent people suffer while, it often seems, bad ones achieve worldly success. I do not know why the COVID-19 virus spread worldwide, wreaking havoc on so many people's lives and the economy. Or why a police officer in Minneapolis held his knee on George Floyd's neck for nearly nine minutes, killing him and causing months of chaos and violence across America. Or why the Holocaust occurred and Adolph Hitler succeeded in plunging the world into the nightmare of World War II. Or why a massive tornado roared through Western Kentucky in 2021, killing people and destroying thousands of homes and businesses, including many in my hometown. Evil has always existed, but I believe that God is good and loving, and he has a plan for everyone. Even though he has not healed me of my paralysis, he has done many amazing things for me.

Using the gifts that God has given me, I am very driven, and I will outwork most other people. I learned a long time ago the importance of keeping hope alive. If you take away hope, you take away the reason or purpose to live. Having no hope is the same as acknowledging that nothing will ever change or improve, and if nothing will change, then why even try? I am certainly not the only person who grew up with significant challenges. But when you factor in all the difficulties that I have overcome with God's help, it is a miracle not just that I have survived for as long as I have, but that I have also attained a fair amount of worldly success and enjoy a relatively full and satisfying life. I am not saying that to boast, but to encourage you that since I was able to accomplish what I have, you also have the ability within you to achieve your hopes and dreams.

Out of curiosity, I once asked a statistician who teaches at a university to calculate the odds of someone like me becoming financially successful. The statistician considered many factors of my life—a coal mining accident resulting in quadriplegia; going to college for ten years in a wheelchair and earning four degrees; passing the bar with no real job opportunities (because of the quadriplegia); starting my own law practice and becoming self-reliant enough to give up my Social Security disability benefits and employ one to six employees for over three decades.

Add in variables like growing up in poverty with an alcoholic, abusive father, surviving a tennis ball-size brain tumor, and more challenges and the statistician concluded that the odds of me achieving my present quality of life are approximately one in 3.9 trillion. The bottom line is that each of our lives is a miracle. Life is precious; we are capable of so much more than we realize.

It is easy to forget how amazing our lives are when we focus too much on our individual problems and lose sight of the big picture. When I was in Panama, it occurred to me how so many people live isolated in their own world, just as I have spent most of my life in Kentucky. Too many people fail to see what exists outside of their own culture and they dismiss or disparage those who do not look, or act, or dress, or talk or believe like them. We are all products of our environment and myriad other factors that shape us. Whenever I start to wallow in self-pity, I try to look at the world around me and realize that God has a reason for everything, even if I do not understand it. Why he has not healed me after so many years, I do not know. However, I still believe in his love and mercy and that he has a plan for my life, as he does for everyone. Hope gives us a reason to move forward. Without it, life would be futile. Every morning, no matter how horrible things have gone the day before, I have a fresh perspective and a reason to keep trying. As God tells us in Jeremiah 29:11, *For I know the thoughts I think for you, thoughts of a peace and a hope for you.*

Every day is an adventure—sometimes fun and joyful, other times filled with suffering. Here is how I get through it: I pray, I thank God for the blessings I have, I ask him for comfort during hard times, and sometimes I ask for something nice for myself or someone else. And, yes, I continue to ask for the one miracle I have requested every day since 1977.

Do I wish I had not gone to work in the coal mine that day? Of course. But I try not to dwell on it too much because if I had not been paralyzed, who knows in what other direction my life would have gone? It is interesting to play "what if," but it can also be risky. When you speculate about how much better your life might be if you had made different choices, you should also consider how much worse off you might be. As the old expression goes, *Grass may be greener on the other side, but it's just as hard to mow.*

If I had not become paralyzed, I might have made millions of dollars playing for the Indiana Pacers and retired comfortably in my 30s. On the other hand, I might have been run over by a speeding car while crossing the street outside the arena after a game. If I had continued playing basketball in college, I probably would never have gone to law school, which means I would not later have helped thousands of people avoid foreclosure or get away from an abusive spouse or stay out of jail and get on the right path to a better life. I also would not have met Connie, the love of my life. I might have married an ax murderer, instead!

From the moment we shook hands in my office, back when she came to see me about handling her divorce, I had a positive feeling about Connie. I liked her touch then, and I still do. Whenever I hold her, she relaxes and breathes deeply, which is her way of saying that she is comfortable; she feels secure; she feels loved. I feel the same way.

Even before we started dating, I felt a closeness with Connie I had never felt with any other person. The love I had for my mother and sisters was a very different kind of closeness. Coming from dysfunctional backgrounds, Connie and I understood each other. Even though we have had many disagreements through the years, we have been able to work through them. I appreciate her forthrightness. With Connie, what you see is what you get. She might snap at me if I say something that offends her, but that's how I learn what's hurtful to her. Otherwise, I might think everything is fine when it is not. Connie and I do not necessarily always think alike, but we think jointly. We are two people in one.

Despite the challenges in my life, I feel very blessed. Since 2009, Connie and I have lived in a ranch-style house in Northern Kentucky, which we rehabbed to make wheelchair-friendly with wide doors and accessible kitchen counters, sinks, and a big shower. We installed a state-of-the-art sound system so we can listen to our favorite music in every room. There is an inground swimming pool in the backyard, complete with a manual lift and harness designed to help me in and out of the water when I feel like swimming. By most standards, our home would be considered middle-class, but compared to the ones I lived in as a boy, it is a mansion. The only problem is an occasional stray golf ball that lands in my backyard from the adjoining golf course. I am fine with that, as long as it does not hit me in the head.

Many people speculate about the things they will ask God when they get to Heaven. As curious as I am about life's mysteries, I doubt if I will ask God anything when I see him, because I will be in such awe of his presence that I will simply say to myself, "Dang!" It will be like basking in the most beautiful warmth of contentment, peace, and serenity. However, if I could ask God one question right now, it would be, "Why did you have to make this faith thing so hard, and why do we have to keep repeating things over and over?"

I believe in fate. Some people call it predestination. But it is not absolute. God has a strategy for each of us, but he also allows us to make choices. Part of life's adventure is figuring out the plan and trying to follow it. It would be nice if God spoke to us directly, in a loud, booming voice, so there could be no misunderstanding regarding his wishes, but then there would be no free will; we would just be like robots programmed to perform specific functions, and nothing more. Usually, he speaks to us quietly, in ways we sense but cannot hear audibly. Studying the Bible and praying helps me to distinguish between God's voice and my fallible imagination.

God gives us the freedom to love him or to reject him, to choose our own path, hopefully within his guidelines. I believe God loves me and wants me to prosper and succeed, to get the best out of myself. I am trying to get from Point A to Point Z, using the Bible as my GPS. Despite making a few wrong turns along the way and getting stuck in some trenches, I have managed to get back on the road heading up the mountain. I can't wait to meet Jesus on the other side. I look forward to seeing you there, too.

Ron Adams in his backyard pool. Photo by Dustin Zeller

Ron's Declarations

HEALING

The joy of the Lord is my strength.
"He heals up the brokenhearted and binds up their wounds."
(Psalm 147:3)

I cry out to the Lord and he answers my prayer.
"And the prayer offered in faith will make the sick person well; the Lord will raise him up." (James 5:15)

Jesus suffered for me so that I can live.
"By His wounds, you have been healed." (1 Peter 2:24)

God loves me and wants me to be healthy.
"I pray that you may enjoy good health and that all may go well with you, even as your soul is getting along well." (3 John 1:2)

The Lord is my rock, my strength, my healer.
"Therefore, strengthen your feeble arms and weak knees. Make level paths for your feet, so that the lame may not be disabled, but rather healed." (Hebrews 12:12-13)

I give God all the glory and praise for healing me.
"I will not die but live, and proclaim what the Lord has done."
(Psalm 118:17)

FAITH

I trust that God is turning my situation around and it will have a positive outcome!
"Now faith is being sure of what we hope for and certain of what we do not see." (Hebrews 11:1)

I may not understand how things can change, but I believe that God can change any problem!
"Because of your faith, it will happen." (Matthew 9:29)

God is directing my steps and I trust Him!
"For I know the plans I have for you," declares the Lord. "Plans to prosper you and not to harm you, plans for a future and a hope." (Jeremiah 29:11)

My life is overflowing with the good things of God!
"I have come that they may have life, and have it to the full." (John 10:10)

God can make a way even if I do not see one!
"For nothing is impossible with God." (Luke 1:37)

God loves me and wants me to prosper and succeed!
"Being fully persuaded that God has power to do what he has promised" (Romans 4:21)

SYMPATHY

God has a perfect plan for life and death.
"There is a time for everything, and a season for every activity under heaven: a time to be born and a time to die." (Ecclesiastes 3:1-2)

God gives eternal comfort.
"Even though I will walk through the valley of the shadow of death, I will fear no evil, for you are with me; your rod and your staff, they comfort me." (Psalm 23:4)

God feels my pain and sorrow and comforts me in my darkest hour.

"Blessed are those who mourn, for they will be comforted." (Matthew 5:4)

God hears me when I cry out to Him.

"He will wipe every tear from their eyes. There will be no more death or mourning or crying or pain, for the old order of things has passed away." (Revelation 21:4)

I will rejoice in the house of the Lord forever.

"It is better to go to a house of mourning than to go to a house of feasting, for death is the destiny of every man; the living should take this to heart." (Ecclesiastes 7:2)

God will turn my suffering into joy.

"May the God of hope fill you with all the joy and peace as you trust in him, so that you may overflow with hope by the power of the Holy Spirit." (Romans 15:13)

CONFIDENCE & STRENGTH

I am giving my fears and worries to God and he will provide the peace I need!

"Cast all your anxieties upon the Lord because He cares for you." (1 Peter 5:7)

I can accomplish all things with Jesus by my side!

"I know the Lord is always with me. I will not be shaken, for He is right beside me. (Psalm 16:8)

I will not let other people intimidate me!

"But the Lord is faithful, and He will strengthen and protect you from the evil one." (2 Thessalonians 3:3)

God has given me the confidence I need to believe in myself and to always be filled with hope!

"So do not throw away your confidence; it will be richly rewarded. You need to persevere so that when you have done the will of God, you will receive what He has promised." (Hebrews 10:35-36)

I am a leader, I am persuasive, I am bold, I am determined and I am fearless!

"For as he thinks in his heart, so is he." (Proverbs 23:7)

God is surrounding me with his shield of protection!

"Finally, be strong in the Lord and his mighty power. Put on the full armor of God so that you can take your stand against the devil's schemes." (Ephesians 6:10-11)

WISDOM

I trust God to fill me with His knowledge and wisdom!

"The fear of the Lord is the beginning of knowledge, but fools despise wisdom and discipline. (Proverbs 1:7)

True wisdom comes from trusting Go and asking Him for direction!

"Do not be wise in your own eyes; fear the Lord and shun evil." (Proverbs 3:7)

My life gives honor and glory to God!

"Wisdom is a tree of life to those who embrace her; happy are those who hold her tightly." (Proverbs 3:18)

God has everything to give meaning to my life!

"In him lie hidden all the treasures of wisdom and knowledge." (Colossians 2:3)

Life is a gift from God and I will enjoy it!

"Blessed is the man who finds wisdom, the man who gains understanding." (Proverbs 3:13)

I put my trust and faith into your written word!

"Fear God and keep his commandments, for this is the whole duty of man. For God will bring every deed into judgement, including every hidden thing, whether it is good or evil." (Ecclesiastes 12:13-14)

CANCER

I am healthy, strong and victorious!

Thanks be to God! He gives us the victory through our Lord Jesus Christ. (1 Corinthians 15:57)

I have an abundance of energy!

"But those who hope in the Lord will renew their strength." (Isaiah 40:31)

God is in control and he has a great plan and future for my life!

"Trust in the Lord with all your heart and lean not on your own understanding." (Proverbs 3:5)

I am at peace with the changes my body is going through!

"And the peace of God, which transcends all understanding, will guard your hears and your minds in Christ Jesus." (Philippians 4:7)

My body is restored to perfect health as my God created it!

"Therefore I tell you, whatever you ask for in prayer, believe that you have received it, and it will be yours." (Mark 11:24)

I am strong and confidant and I will defeat this cancer!

"I can do all things through Christ who gives me strength." (Philippians 4:13)

FINANCES

My past is wiped away and I have a new beginning!
"I will repay you for the years the locusts have eaten." (Joel 2:25)

I am making wise decisions with my money.
"Do your planning and prepare your fields before building your house." (Proverbs 24:27)

When I put God first, all of my needs are satisfied!
"I know what it is to be in need, and I know what it is to have plenty. I have learned the secret of being content in any and every situation, whether well fed or hungry, whether living in plenty or in want." (Philippians 4:12)

I will keep pressing forward and never give up!
"For God did not gives us a spirit of timidity, but a spirit of power, of love and of self-discipline." (2 Timothy 1:7)

I am successful, I am talented, and I am blessed!
"But remember the Lord your God, for it is he who gives you the ability to produce wealth!" (Deuteronomy 8:18)

With God, I will accomplish all of my goals and dreams!
"By his mighty power at work within us, he is able to accomplish infinitely more than we would ever dare to ask or hope for." (Ephesians 3:20)

DEPRESSION

I am happy, positive, and victorious!
"A righteous man may have many troubles, but the Lord delivers him from them all." (Psalm 34:19)

I trust that God has a special plan for my life!

"And we know that in things God works for the good of those who love him, who have been called according to his purpose." (Romans 8:28)

I will cherish every moment that makes me smile!

"This is the day the Lord has made; let us rejoice and be glad in it." (Psalm 118:24)

I am thankful for the people God has put in my life!

"Every time I think of you, I give thanks to my God." (Philippians 1:3)

I will forget the past and look forward to the future!

"I press on toward the goal to win the prize for which God has called me heavenward in Christ Jesus." (Philippians 3:14)

I will take back my life and defeat depression!

"I can do all things through Christ who gives me strength." (Philippians 4:13)

ACKNOWLEDGMENTS

Acknowledgments are like wedding invitations—some people who probably should be included will almost certainly be left out, only to be remembered after it is too late. Countless friends and colleagues have helped and inspired me in so many ways. I would like to mention a few, but to those whose names I am forgetting at this moment, please accept my sincere apology and know that I am grateful for your involvement in my life.

First, I would like to thank my wife, Connie Adams, for her unconditional love and friendship. When it comes to Connie, my only regret is that it took so long to meet her, but she was certainly worth the wait. Thanks, also, to my sons Joe and Rick for the joy and pleasure they have brought me through the years, especially Rick, for the quality time that we shared together throughout his childhood and teenage years, and still do.

I must also thank my mother, Ruth Adams, for teaching me right from wrong early in life and for her selfless love and sacrifices to provide me with a happy childhood, despite the many hardships she faced. Thanks to my sisters, Joyce Boucher and Deloris "Lolo" Hinton, for always being there for me when I was a child and for their invaluable support and encouragement, especially during the early years following my accident. I would also like to thank my half-sister, Sherry Smith, for her friendship, even though it was, regrettably, a long-distance relationship. Thanks to my brother-in-law, Richard Hinton (Lolo's husband), for helping me in so many ways, and my brother-in-law Roger Drake (Sherry's husband), for his godly inspiration.

Thanks to my teachers at Dawson Springs High School for putting up with me before I became a good student. Thanks to my basketball coach, Norman Manasco, for believing in me and for instilling the athletic discipline I needed to become a better player.

So many medical professionals have helped me recover from physical and psychological wounds through the years. First and foremost, I want to thank Craig Hospital for teaching me that I still had a life worth living and that it could be fun and for showing me how being a quadriplegic does not have to mean being confined to a bed. I will never forget how Dr. Ward Curtis and his staff woke me early every morning and got me into a regular routine, making me feel like a real person again. I especially want to single out Adele Stalder, my first physical therapist at Craig, and Jan Brabant, an amazing recreational therapist. Their positive attitude was as important as the technical and medical information that they taught me. Closer to home, I have dealt with countless doctors and therapists, but one who has been especially helpful is Dr. Stephen Heis, M.D., a Physical Medicine & Rehabilitation Specialist in Cincinnati.

Thanks to Cincinnati Children's Hospital for their extraordinary treatment of my son, Joe, and for getting him back on his feet following his spinal stroke as a teenager.

Thanks to the psychiatrist at The Rehabilitation Center in Louisville, Kentucky, who first suggested that maybe I could be a lawyer. Thanks to Chase College of Law for providing the education I needed to become one. Thanks, especially, to law professors Paula Raines and Carol Eisenbard and Dr. Julie Gerdsen of Northern Kentucky University's MBA program. Thanks to David Massamore for giving me my first job as a lawyer.

Of course, I would not still be an attorney without the tireless help of Bernie Zeller, my vice president of operations, Elena Wellman, my financial paralegal, and Melanie Holton, my receptionist, who makes everyone who walks through the door of my office feel wonderful.

Thanks to the late and brilliant Dr. Tim Alexander, who was my pastor at Florence Baptist Church in Union, Kentucky, for his wisdom; to Pastor Brian Tome of Crossroads Community Church in Cincinnati for his spiritual leadership; to Marcus Mecum, senior pastor at 7 Hills Church in Florence, Kentucky, for his guidance. Thanks to Joel Osteen for keeping me motivated through his many powerful sermons and inspirational books. Thanks to his mother, Dodie Osteen, for her friendship.

Finally, I would like to thank God for teaching me that love is the greatest gift we have and can share and for sending his Son, Jesus Christ, to set an example for the world and save us from our sins. Without Him, I would be nothing. With Him, I am everything. I pray that you find the same peace and happiness.

W. Ron Adams holds a bachelor's degree in Business Administration from Murray State University and a JD/MBA from the Salmon P. Chase College of Law at Northern Kentucky University. As a lawyer, he focuses primarily on bankruptcy, family, disability and personal injury law. Before becoming a lawyer, he was a coal miner, a homebuilder and owner of a carwash. He resides in Northern Kentucky with his wife and several dogs.

Fred Anderson is a former journalist who worked as a reporter, writer and news producer at several radio and television stations. He has also freelanced as a field producer for several television shows including *America's Most Wanted, Inside Edition, Extra!* and more. He is currently a public relations consultant for musicians, comedians and filmmakers. One of his most memorable projects was promoting William Shatner's country music album *Why Not Me* and the actor's subsequent Grand Ole Opry debut with Jeff Cook of the band Alabama.